JAPANESE
SPA RESORTS

Edited by Jinling Qu
Translated by Weinan Dai

DESIGN MEDIA PUBLISHING LIMITED

Contents

1

Shimoda Yamatokan

Location: 2048 Kisami, Shimoda, Shizuoka Prefecture, 415-0028, Japan

Spa Name: Shimoda Onsen

Area: 17,284 m^2

Quantity of Guest Room: 60

Quantity of Spa Facilities: 8

Located in Tatado Beach, Shimoda, Shizuka Prefecture, Shimoda Spa perfectly combines Japanese style with natural conditions of the surrounding mountains and sea, making it a cosy and comfortable bathing paradise. Apart from the convenience brought by the modern luxury guest rooms, open-air bathing pools and the dinning rooms, the guests can also indulge themselves in the natural environment with bamboo forest, pine trees, reed mat and Shigaraki Ceramic – the dramatic and organic amalgamation of spa bath and nature, bringing them to the pure nature. With the unique modelling of light and shadow and its transparent visual effect, the design of the spa integrates the beauty of Tatado Beach and the rolling hills, creating a surreal world.

All guest rooms are set within villas with terraces. Guests can overlook the blue sea, whether from the guest rooms or the outdoor bathing pool or even the dinning area.

The fourth floor features the large bathroom named "Paradise View" in which the guest have a bath facing the sea in the ocean-front western-style large bath and the open-air bathtub. All guests can indulge themselves in all the facilities here upon arrival to departure.

The guests can enjoy the characteristic seafood feast "Umi No Sachi" and "Yama No Sachi" in the guest room or in the dinning room, or even enjoy the charcoal fire barbecue in the dinning room.

1. The panorama of Shimoda Yamatokan. Located in the natural world of surrounding mountains and sea in southern Izu, the hotel enjoys a panoramic view of the beautiful white Tatado Beach

2. "Kirara", Japanese mountaintop open-air bath

3. The panorama of Shimoda Yamatokan

4. Guest room with private open-air bath which is made of the well-known Japanese Shigaraki Ceramic

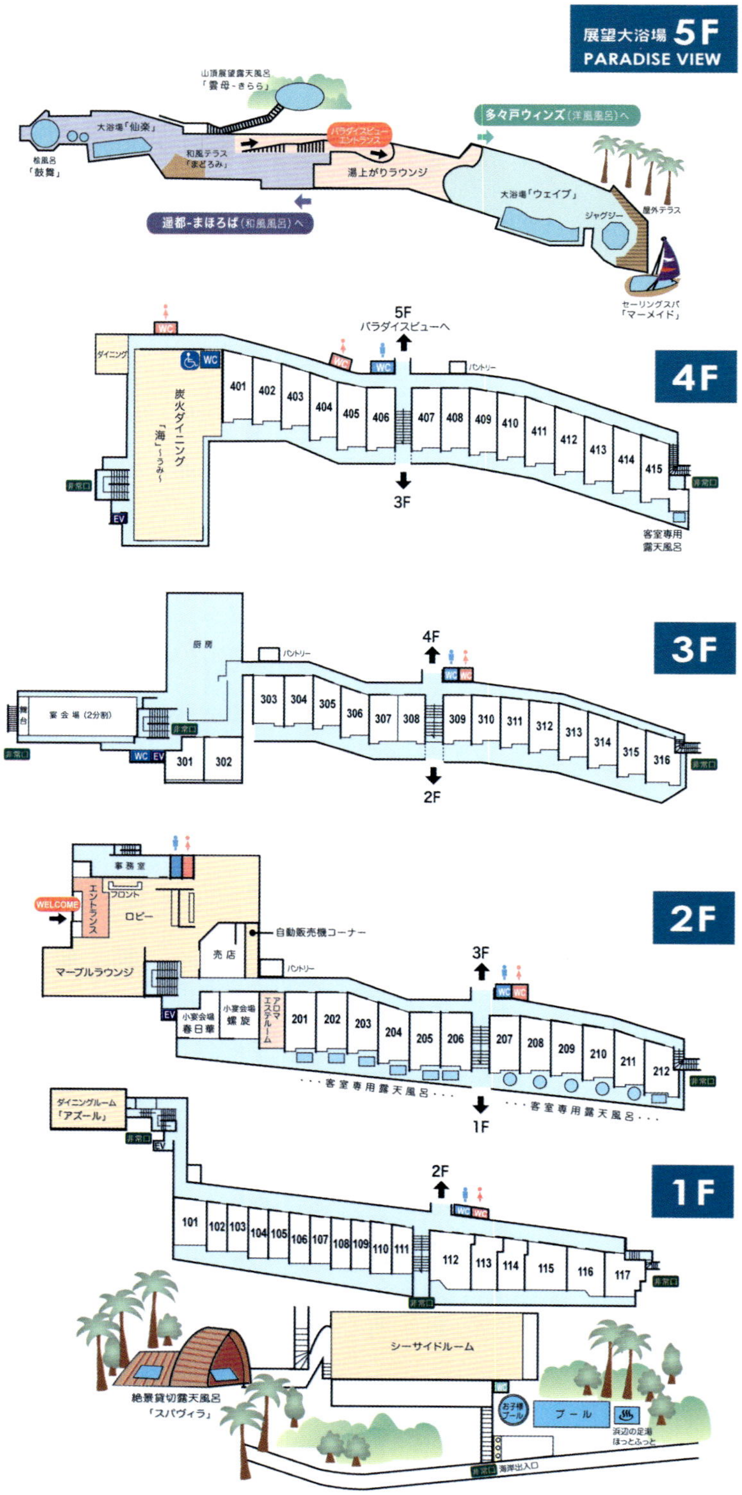

5

5. plan

3

4

I like the little garden under
the patio. A little too barren,
needs better plants. But the
idea is wonderful. Adds
a nice touch to the minimalistic
look on the ~~bath~~ balcony.

6

7

6. Private outdoor bath "PINE"

7. Private open-air bath "PINE", featuring the impressive hemisphere-shape roof and the representative pine among the surrounding plants

8. Private outdoor bath "BAMBOO", set within the exotic environment with the surrounding bamboos. The outdoor bath is equipped with special night lighting system.

10

11

9. The most popular guest room 212 and its private outdoor pool equipped with special lighting system

10. Guest room 212

11. Japanese and Oriental style guest room

1

Otsuki Hotel Wafuukan

Location: 3-19 Higashikaigancho, Atami, Shizuoka Prefecture 413-0012, Japan

Spa Name: Atami Onsen

Area: 2,640 m^2

Quantity of Guest Room: 24

Quantity of Spa Facilities: 6

Otsuki Hotel Wafuukan was designed with the motif of "Sanctuary for Adults", therefore it is so appropriate to describe the Japanese spa hotel as a paradise hidden from the city. Located in the downtown area of Atami, Otsuki Hotel Wafuukan Spa boasts the precious tranquility and cosiness. Opposite the vestibule with a lattice door is the spacious room in Japanese style. It also features the Koya Maki Tree open-air bath and the stone bath, made of the 300-year-old superior ancient cypress and the indoor spa bath where guests can catch sight of the green patio through the transparent vertical glass. It was a favourite place of the Tokugawa's. Tourists can go over the interesting history, experiencing wonderful Japanese culture. It is only two minutes' walk to the Atami Sun Beach bathing spot, which makes the hotel more attractive.

The original Japanese teahouse-style spaces, guest rooms in different styles and the Kaiseki Cuisine, which is full of reminiscent mood to Japanese history help guests escape from the hustle and bustle of city life to feel the pure tranquility with time passing by.

Both breakfast and lunch can be enjoyed in the guest room. The Japanese Kaiseki Cuisine select fresh local vegetables and seafood and carefully cooked by the chef.

靜觀

1. The night scene of the vestibule

2. The corridor permeated with Japanese culture

3-4. The Koya Madi Tree spa bathroom – the luxurious independent spa bath made of the ancient cypress which is more than 300 years old

4

3

5

6

5. The Koya Madi Tree spa bathroom, providing Fujisawa no Yu that exhumed from its own properties, once enjoyed by the Tokugawa family, is one of the famous spas in Japan.

6. The indoor spa bath where the guests can catch sight of the green patio through the transparent vertical glass

7. The luxurious lounge surrounded by the bamboo garden and pond, outpouring tranquility from its dynamic design

8. The guest room with open-air spa

9

9. Japanese guest room decorated in traditional Japanese colours

10. Guest room in both Japanese and European style, whose transparent design affords a direct view of the garden

Seizanyamato

Location: 203 OkaIto-City Shizouka Prefecture, 414-0055, Japan

Spa Name: Ito Onsen

Area: 8,220 m^2

Quantity of Guest Room: 42

Nestled on the serene and amicable hillside in Ito City, Shizuoka Prefecture, it is an up-to-date Japanese hotel. Taking advantage of the unique topography of Ito, the designer created a paradise on earth, connecting mountains and rivers amidst the overlapping peaks and knolls with use of natural materials such as bamboo, wood, reed, tatami, sliding window and screen. The Japanese architecture technology and wisdom demonstrated here make guests intoxicated in the comfortable and cosy spa.

Seizanyamato provides private open-air baths and rentable spas service. It boasts 42 rooms in total, among which there are 5 high-grade guest rooms with private open-air pool and 2 suites with open-air baths. All the spa facilities, including separate large spa pools for men and women, the outdoor spa bathing spots and the exclusive hourly bathtubs, adopt the water circulating system. The guests can lie in the spa admiring the sparkling stars in the sky at night and overlook the sea far away during daytime with the rippling sound of the running spring nearby .

There are also such supporting facilities as stores, beauty salons, recreation rooms, karaoke clubs and lounges in which you are free to surf the internet. Here serves the custom-made dish menu updated every month, among which the most popular one is the elaborate Kaiseki Cuisine cooked with exquisite ingredients, featuring Seizanyamato flavour.

There are three choices respectively for drinks, entrée and dessert in the Japanese cuisine called "Seizan Kaiseki Ryori", the ones can be chosen in accordance with personal taste.

1. The night view of the façade – one corner of the colourful and dazzling yard in the dim light of night

2.The overall view of Seizanyamato

3. The cosy and comfortable lobby

4. The large bath "Tsuki no Yu". At "Tsuki no Yu", you can enjoy a far view of the Ito streets and the water and sky of one hue of Sagami bay.

5. The night view of the vestibule. Blooming Oshima Sakura can be seen around the vestibule in February every year.

3

4

6

7

8

6. The open-air bath "Kaze no Yu", covered with mist and water, makes you feel like standing high in the clouds.

7. The open-air bath "Hoshi no Yu" is an open-air stone spa in the face of mountains and woods, running over with the amorous feelings of mountains. The guests can enjoy the sparkling stars all over the sky at night, lying comfortably in the spa.

8. Teahouse, where you can enjoy the cosy space by overlooking the green view through the large window while leisurely tasting the fragrant flavour of tea

9

10

9. The lounge for after-bath, providing various drinks such as pure water and purple Perilla juice which are prepared in the changing rooms which radiate the unique flavour of wood. The guests can also see the green plants in the patio, while regaining physical strength.

10. The beauty salon "Kirakira", where the guests enjoy the massage with natural vanilla essential oil amidst the vanilla smell permeating the inside space

11. The standard guest room, equipped with natural-material-made tatamis, sliding windows and screens, showcasing the Japanese architectural technology and wisdom

Hotel MICURAS

Location: 3-19, Higashikaigancho, Atami, Shizuoka Prefecture, 413-0012, Japan

Spa Name: Atami Onsen

Area: 1,320 m^2

Quantity of Guest Room: 62

Quantity of Spa Facilities: 4

Hotel MICURAS is located in Sagami Bay, adjacent to Atami beach. Taking advantage of the beautiful beach landscape of Sagami Bay, the designer created sea-view spa pools. The concept was inspired from illimitable sea & sky, and employed blue and white as the main furnishing colours. MICURAS incorporates the bath and wellness services, which had attracted all-aged customers. The spa service, which had been focusing on health care as its main service item, has won good reputation among tourists of all age group, especially the female guests, since its opening in January, 2007. The most brilliant touch goes to the panoramic open spa, where guests can enjoy different sceneries from the ocean front spa which has a panoramic view of the whole peninsular, to the wonderful neighbourhood and night scene of the sand beach, which can be seen directly by lying in the spa bathing pool. In sunny days, an overall view of the whole peninsula can be enjoyed in the spa where bathing seems like swimming in the sea.

2

1. Hotel MICURAS on the Atami Beach in warm sea wind

2. Open ocean front communal spa bath III, where one can catch sight of the beautiful neighbourhood and the night scene of the Atami sun beach

3. Open ocean front communal spa bath II. It has a transparent view from the interior to the outside. The hot spring here can improve your skin to be smoother and gentler.

4. The corridor of men's exclusive lounge

5. Open-air ocean front large spa pool with a commanding view of Sagami Bay, Hatsushima and Oshima

3

4

6. The luxurious suites for honeymoon, open-view pool provides a panoramic view of the seascape

7. The panoramic view of the restaurant, where the hazy candle light combined with the leisurely music will accompany you for dinner time

8

8. The overall scene of the MICURAS Café, which locates along the seaside, offering a cosy environment for enjoyable afternoon tea

9. The guest room with indoor bath pool

10. The MICURAS Suite with spacious living room

11. The luxurious ocean-view guest room. There are luxurious private ocean front bath pools, high-tech beauty and spa facilities. The spacious living room, bedrooms as well as the beautiful seascape make you fully intoxicated in the incomparable holiday

12. The night scene of the MICURAS Suite, with ocean-view spa pool

11

12

1

The Prince Hakone Resort

Location: 144 Motonhakone, Hakone-machi, Ashigara-shimo-gun, Kanagawa, 250-0592, Japan

Spa Name: Lake Ashi Takokawa Onsen

Area: 94,500 m^2

Quantity of Guest Room: 138 (Main building 94; Annexe 44)

Quantity of Spa Facilities: 4

The Prince Hakone Resort has two famous spas in Hakone: Kohan Spa and Yumedono Onsen with hot spring coming from Takokawa Onsen, one of the top seventeen spas in Hakone. The Lakeside Spa in the Prince Hakone boasts the natural advantage of spas and the adjoining mountains and rivers, enjoying a commanding view of Mount Fuji and adjacent Lake Ashi. Mount Fuji endows the spa with enchanting glamour in all seasons of a year. The Prince Hakone Resort is the flagship store of the Prince Grand Hotel and Resorts Group. Guests here can enjoy the comfortable holiday time and the infinite space in harmony with nature, intoxicating in such warm embrace of Lake Ashi and Hakone mountains and forget to leave. The open-air spa against the natural beauty of lakes and mountains provides the guests with the delight in the gentle sunshine and the lake landscape. Guests can totally soothe their mind and body by overlooking Mount Fuji from Lake Ashi. The spa here is rich in the natural elements such as calcium, sodium, sulfate and chloride, which have the significant effects in curing neuralgia, myalgia and arthralgia, and moreover can relax the muscles, stimulate the blood circulation and alleviate travelling fatigue.

1. Fuji Mount at the Hakone lakeside

2. Fuji Mount behind Nakaniwa Lake with implicit and charming beauty just like a shy and pretty girl playing pipa

3. The open-air spa adjacent to lakes and mountains

4. The indoor spa pool

5

5. The exterior view of the Prince Hakone Resort

3

4

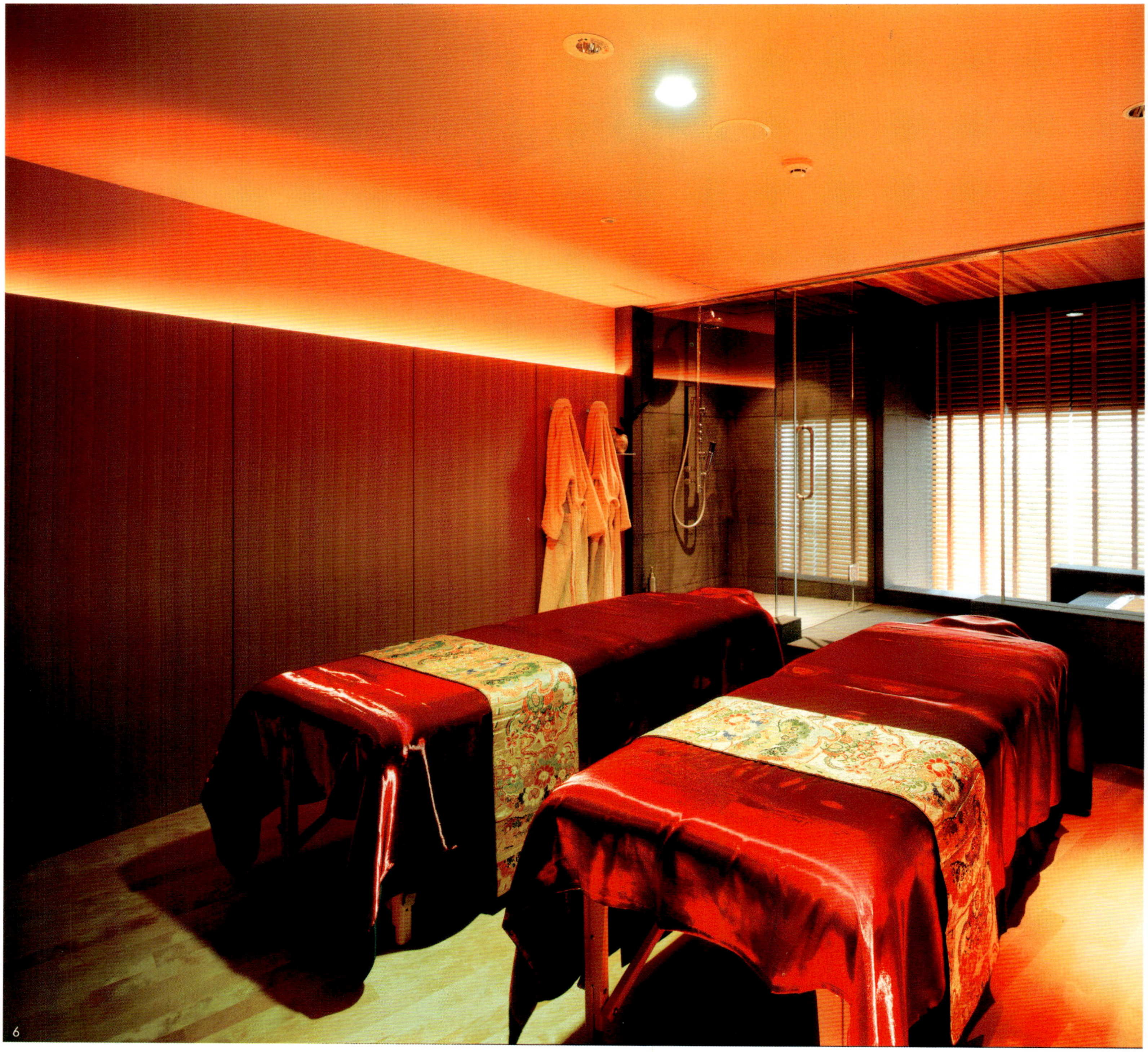
6

6. The massage room

7. One of the guest rooms, boasting gentle sunshine and lake view

8. The guest room in the annexe

7

8

1

Ootaki Hotel

Location: 750 – 1 Miyakami, Yugawara-machi, Ashigarashimo-gun, Kanagawa Prefecture, 259-0314, Japan

Spa Name: Yugawara Onsen

Area: 20,955 m^2

Quantity of Guest Room: 43

Quantity of Spa Facilities: 5

Ootaki Hotel possesses one of the largest volumes of hot spring water in the Yugawara hot spring resort and is located adjacent to the picturesque Fudou-taki(Fudou Waterfall). As one of the rare natural onsen resorts with rich soil and resource in suburban Tokyo, it boasts comprehensive range of hot spring facilities including open-air bath with views of surrounding landscape, hot spring swimming pool that can be used all year round, swimming-wear-required rooftop bath and foot onsen, while it takes most pride in the open-air baths which not only command a view of the famous Fudou Waterfall but enjoy the most plentiful hot spring volume. It features seasonal Japanese Kaiseki Ryori created with local vegetables and sea food. Hotel has installed wheelchair slope at the entrance and lift capable for accommodating wheelchairs. Hotel has also established barrier free rooms and handrails in open-air bath.

1. The façade of the eight-storey building with hot spring water supply for all the rooms

2. The open-air spa bath "Kanontaki no Yu", swimwear-required for both men and women

3. The foot bath "Kanon"

4. The open-air spa bath "Kanontaki no Yu"

5. The surrounding attraction of the famous "Fudou-taki" of Yugawara Onsen

3

4

6

7

8

6. The outdoor spa of "Taki no Yu"
7. The outdoor spa of "Hotaru no Yu"
8. The indoor pool "Taki no Yu"

9. The indoor pool "Hotaru no Yu" with the top-class hot spring from Yugawara Onsen, whose rich volume brims the Kitakami stone bath

10. The exlusive cpen-air spa in the guest room

11. The hot spring swimming pool, which is available all year round

10
11

12

12. One of the guest rooms with open-air bath

13. The standard Japanese-style guest room

14. One of the Western-style guest rooms

13

14

1

Hakone Washintei Hougetsu

Location: 90-42 Hakone, Hakone, Asigarasimogun, Kanagawa Prefecture, 250-0522, Japan

Spa Name: Lake Ashi Onsen

Area: approx. 4,000 m^2

Quantity of Guest Room: 15

Quantity of Spa Facilities: 4

The name of the hotel Hakone Hougetu comes from the beautiful full moon views in Hakone Mountain with the central theme of moon. The ideal location on the mound enables guests to admire the vivid song of birds and overlook the stunning seasonal landscape of Lake Ashi. The interior decoration everywhere set off the poetic imagery of full moon such as the "Fugetu no Yu", "Tsukimi no Yu" and "Deai Tsuki no Yu", pursuing a kind of simple and elegant mood and spirit, which implies the dream for the natural elements in Japanese culture whilst presents the guests the comfortable and cosy private space. Whether in the open-air common bath or the private exclusive bath, guests can enjoy themselves in high-quality sulfurous hot spring of Lake Ashi Onsen while admiring the splendid starry sky.

Equipped with "Hori–Kotatsu" (low heated table with legroom built into the floor), the spacious rooms with varied layouts create a sense of openness. The Japanese Ryotei restaurant with private rooms has been serving seasonal cuisine with monthly updated menu since its opening. Guests can enjoy the pleasure of tasting the exclusive cuisine cooked with local ingredients and admiring the stunning scenery of Hakone at the same time.

1. The hotel with the central theme of "Tsuki", attracted by the angelic image "Hougetu" in Hakone

2. The typical Japanese hotel, named in odd number

3. The "Yukemuri Tsuki" indoor bathing pool with the natural screen through large windows

4. The "Tsukimi no Yu" outdoor bathing pool

5. The "Fugetu no Yu"

6. The "Deai Tsuki no Yu" bathing pool in the form of a bathtub made of high-grade cypress

7. The modern-style chartered bath, focusing on the private space

8. The indoor bath pool presents a different feeling by bathing in the rounded bathing pool and admiring the moon and stars through the window

9. The design element demonstrates the owner's adoration to moon

8

9

10

11

12

10. The corridor to the reception hall whose design focuses on the creation of the Japanese beauty with natural ornaments

11. The reading room for guests' leisure time, equipped with massage armchairs

12. The reception hall where you can catch sight of the stunning scenery of Lake Ashi and the surrounding landscape

13. The Japanese-style guest rooms which command a panoramic view of Lake Ashi

14. Various room layouts according to the quantity of guests

15 The private room in the restaurant

14

15

1

Gora Tensui

Location: 1320-276 Gora, Hakone, Ashigarashimogun, Kanagawa Prefecture, Japan

Spa Name: Hakone Gora Onsen

Area: 2,775 m^2

Quantity of Guest Room: 14

Quantity of Spa Facilities: 4

Other Facilities: "Ashiyu" Café; Rock Base Bath; Sauna and Esthetics Salon

It takes only one minute to walk to Gora Tensui after getting off from the mountain train at Gora Station. Incorporating the modern and traditional Japanese architectural style to the whole design, the design of the guest room emphasises the privacy as well as the ornamental characters. The ideal location affords six sightseeing choices. The guests can catch sight of the grand occasion of the Hakone traditional culture ceremony, "Daimonji Matsuri" and overlook "Mt. Myojogatake" in Hakone Izu National Park. It also boasts the elegant surrounding landscape such as the splendid flower sea of plum blossom and sakura in early spring, the fragrant blossoming lilac in midsummer, the fiery maple leaf layers all over the mountain in early autumn and the snow-coated tress in winter.

Acidity defines the quality of hot springs here, and there are milky white salt elements with acidity in the water of "Bansui no Yu" and "Sansui no Yu". This kind of element, blended with the alkalinity of human cells, can develop the effect of relieving fatigue and defusing the vivotoxin. The exclusive bath and the rock base bath are free. There are also irregularly scheduled culture exhibitions of each and every kind.

1. The night scene of the entrance

2. The contracted open-air bath named "Myojogatake no Yu" which can be used without reservation. Somma in Hakone is right under your nose when you bathe in the open-air bath.

3. The night scene of the natural hot spring "Bansui no Yu"

4. The open-air spa of the Japanese guest room "Suisei"

5. The vestibule with a direct access to the most representative "Ashiyu" Café

3

4

6-7. The "Ashiyu" Café "Mastuyoi". You can enjoy the first welcome drink as complimentary while having your weary feet sank in the hot spring.

8

9

8. The Japanese and Western-style guest room "Suien" with private open-air bath, creating the modern and traditional atmosphere with the amenities of the high-grade "Ryukyu Tatami" and the low bed design

9. The standard guest room with the high-grade "Sulphur Tatami", totalling 12 tatami mat (20 square metres), together with a small-size living room and a shower

10. The Japanese guest room named "Suikei" totalling 12 tatami mat (20 square metres) plus 7.5 tatami mat (12 square metres)

1

Hotel Kajikaso

Location: 688 Yumoto, Hakone-machi, Ashigarashimo-gun, Kanagawa, Japan

Spa Name: Hakone Yumoto Onsen

Area: about 9,900 m^2

Quantity of Guest Room: 74

Capacity: 430 persons

Spa Facilities: Indoor sap pool 2, outdoor spa 8 in 5 types and foot spa

It takes only five minutes to walk to Hotel Kajikaso after getting off the train at Hakone Yumoto Station. The designer of the hotel took full advantages of all the spaces of the spa. There is an observatory large communal spa bath named "Seiryuu no Yu" on the roof terrace on the fifth floor and an open-air spa "Soun no Yu" on the first floor. The spa services are available to men and women at different time intervals. There are nine spas in total with rich water volume. The elegant surrounding environment commanding a panoramic view of the stunning seasonal landscape of Hakone Mount, makes guests feel at ease, which is also the main idea of the hotel. On the wooden deck on the first floor, guests can take a rest by having a foot spa and enjoy the natural oxygen bar, while listening to the rippling sound of the running brook. The hotel is also equipped with various public recreational amenities such as Karaoke Hall, Mahjong Hall and Banquet Hall in different sizes. With the good reputation of "Home of Kajikaso's Food", the hotel offers exceptional Japanese cuisine cooked with fresh seafood from Sagami Bay.

There are a large number of tourist attractions around, namely, river fishing, tennis court, golf, hiking, mountain-climbing, mountain vegetables picking, museum, aquarium, botanical garden and art gallery.

1. The façade of the typical Japanese hotel facing Hayakawa

2. The large open-air communal bath named "Soun no Yu". "Soun no Yu" on the first floor is for men exclusively.

3. Outdoor spa pool named "Tsukimi no Yu"

4. The foot bath. The fatigue of the feet is relieved.

5. The four observatory communal spas "Hoshimi no Yu"

3

4

6

6. The lounge named "Keiryuu"

7. The lounge of the ante chamber named "Fuga"

8

9

8-9. The Japanese guest room with the layout of 20-square-metre interior and an outdoor spa, which has a room capacity of 6 persons, suitable for the family tour

10. The Japanese and Western style guest room "Syusuian", with a 16-square-metre interior, a living room and an outdoor spa facing the stream

Yushintei

Location: 193 Yumoto, Ashigarashimo-gun, Kanagawa Prefecture, Japan

Spa Name: Hakone Yumoto Onsen

Area: 953.32 m^2

Quantity of Guest Room: 10

Quantity of Spa Facilities: 5

Yushintei is based in the tourist attraction of Yumoto, Hakone, Kanto, Japan. It is only one kilometre away from Hakone Yumoto Staion. Fifteen to twenty minutes' walk along the Skumogawa River towards Tasidoori Onsen Town can lead you to the destination in the deep lane of the hotel street, which endows the spa with the lingering charm, profound and lasting, small but exquisite. It is a two-storey building in wooden structure. The Kiasian on the ground floor with open-air spas are named as "Kisaian Ai", "Kisaian Kohaku", "Kisaian Toki" and "Kiasian Sawarabi". The modern-style design with private open-air spa offers guests a feeling of absolute privacy.

The natural alkaline water of Yushintei Spa can not only relax the muscles and stimulate the blood circulation but exert unique function in maintaining beauty image for the female. The tranquility and the considerate and thoughtful service make guests intoxicated in the ultimate relaxation and enjoyment of splendid holiday time.

1. The entrance façade of Yushintei, gentle and cosy

2. The exclusive stone spa, rentable by hour

3. One corner of the vestibule inside, in the simple and gentle style

4. Ryokuin, where the guest can enjoy the green view of the courtyard while enjoying the spa

5. The vestibule and the front desk, mostly decorated with Japanese paper, creating an atmosphere of a warm home in the gentle light

3

4

6. The open-air spa bath in the guest room "Kisaian Kohaku"

7. The open-air spa bath in the guest room "Kisaian Ai", a wooden spa pool in subtropical style

8. The guest room with Japanese feelings, enjoying the beauty of nature

9. The restaurant and typical wooden desktop in semi-closed style

10. The guest room "Kisaian Kohaku"

9

10

Kamogawakan

Location: 1179 Nishi-cho, Kamogawa City, Chiba Prefecture, Japan

Spa Name: Kamogawa Onsen

Area: 18,915.7 m^2

Quantity of Guest Room: 65

Quantity of Spa Facilities: 20

Located in the south of Boso Peninsula, Kanto, Kamogawakan enjoys a warm and pleasant seasonal climate. Facing the Pacific Ocean, Kamogawn is constructed in a simple but elegant Sukiya-zukuri style building structure amidst the surrounding pine trees (Sukiya-zukuri style building structure is a Japanese architectural style, featuring a main building whose façade looks like a teahouse and a courtyard). There are 17 spa pools inside the capacious space including a rooftop footbath "Haruka" commanding a splendid view of the Pacific Ocean. Various types of guest rooms are available here such as the standard Japanese-style, the mixed style of Japanese and Western-style, the ones for lovers and the ones with exclusive open-air baths, whilst the most outstanding guest room goes to the one on the top floor which has the picturesque scenery.

Boso Peninsula has long been crowned as the treasure-house of marine products. Thus, the seafood here is always fresh and delicious. Kamogawakan specialises in serving local seafood which is made of ingredients from Kamogawa, in order to maximise the freshness of the dishes. The open kitchen presents guests a freindly and dynamic feeling.

2

3

1. The façade of the onsen hotel in the graceful architectural style

2. The bubble bath for men, an octagon bathing pool with the smell of cypress

3. Enjoying the splendid seascape of the Pacific Ocean while having a foot spa

4. The large bathing pool in men's spa

5. The large bathing pool of women's spa, among which there are three bathing pools with different temperatures that can be chosen according to personal body condition

6

6. The open-air bath in the guest room, facing the sea

4

5

7. Massage and therapy hall

8. Standard Japanese suite including one Japanese guest room with 10 tatamis mat (16.2 square metres) and two Japanese guest rooms with 4.5 tatamis mat (7.29 square metres)

9. Standard guest room, mixed Japanese and Western style

8

9

Amagisou

Location: 359 Nashimoto, Kawazu-cho, Kamo-gun, Shizuoka Prefecture, Japan

Spa Name: Oodaru Onsen

Area: 500,000 m^2

Quantity of Guest Room: 44

Quantity of Spa Facilities: 37 in 28 types

Sited in the central area of Izu Peninsula in Kanto, Amagisou is crowned as one of the most famous hot springs in Japan. Occupying 500,000-square- metre site, it was built along the Kawazu River, featuring the open-air bath "Kawara no Yu" which commands a panoramic view of the best-known "Otaki", one of the top seven great waterfalls in Kawazu. The stunning scenery of nature, together with numerous grand indoor spas of various kinds throughout the garden, constitutes an unmatched spa kingdom. Besides the picturesque "Kawara no Yu", the ryokan also boasts the 30-metre-deep "Hidden Cave Spa Bath", the metal bathtub heated from beneathwith typical Japanese characteristics, "Kodakara no Yu" which may bless you to have many sons and grandsons after bathing in it and "25-metre Hot Spring Swimming Pool" which is available in all seasons. The experiences of viewing flower blossoms in Spring, snow sightseeing in Winter, admiring stars in the sky at night and listening to sounds of the natural fields, being a part of the natural mountains and rivers, make guests enjoy themselves so much as to forget to leave.

There are as many as 28 spa pools such as indoor pools, open-air baths, cave baths, waterfall bath, spa baths (available in winter), stone baths and family baths, which may take guests several days to experience them all.

温泉天国
天城

1. The panoramic view of the Japanese architecture in the vilage

2. The open-air bath named "Kawara no Yu". There are totally five pools in dfferent temperatures, which can be chosen according to individual body condition. Being a part of the valley, it is an imaginary experience to bathe in the water mist sprayed from Odaru Waterfall.

3. "Dousojin no Yu", the hot spring bath with shallow stream, the ideal bath for admiring the beautiful natural scenery

4

4. Women's open-air bath, which has a panoramic view of the blooming sakura in February every year

3

5. The indoor pool for men called "Iwa Buro", which was built of the local rock of Amagi

6. View from half-open bath pool for women, in which you can overlook the red maples, green trees and mountains, bringing you a pleasant mood

7. The indoor bath pool for women

8. The indoor bath pool for men equipped with "Kodakara no Yu", "Herbal Medicine Bath", and the like

9

9. The open-air bath pool in the special guest room

10. The balcony of the guest room. Most of the building materials come from the local wood in Amagi, creating a natural sense.

11. View to the outside from the balcony of the guest room

12. The restaurant named "Wakatake", with comfortable seats, capacious dinning space and the open kitchen which offers various kinds of freshly cooked cuisine, including the diversified Japanese buffet breakfast

13. The banquet hall which can accommodate 120 persons, equipped with a stage and the professional acoustic equipments

12

13

1

Mizuniwa no Hatago Sumiyoshikan

Location: 1149-1, Kona, Izunokuni City, Shizuoka 410-2201, Japan

Spa Name: Kona Onsen

Area: 2,549.53 m^2

Quantity of Guest Room: 20

Quantity of Spa Facility: 4

Other Facilities: private open-air bath, rentable open-air bath

Sitting on the riverside of Kano River in central Izu Peninsula, Mizuniwa no Hatago Sumiyoshikan is a Japanese hotel permeated with the natural beauty of Izu. The various guest rooms with unique design offer a comfortable and pleasant experience. The hot spring inside the hotel is called Kona Onsen, whose history can be traced back to the Kamakura Period (1185~1333). Kona Onsen boasts spa baths in various styles such as the large stone open-air baths and the chartered open-air baths, "Keika no Yu".

The room "Fugatei" facing Kano River, commanding a panoramic view of the ever-changing scenery in all seasons, is a traditional Japanese guest room where guests can overlook the rolling mountains of Hakone. The annexe named "Retoro", exquisite and elegant, encompasses the traditional sense of beauty and the modern comfort and conciseness. The guest rooms inside the annexe are equipped with the chartered open-air spa baths and Japanese beds.

The food here is the typical Japanese Kaiseki Ryori, elaborately cooked with fishes from Suruga Bay and the fresh seasonal vegetables, which are full of delicious flavour and abundant nutriment.

1. The panoramic view of "Fugatei"

2. The night scene of the tranquil and serene Japanese garden

3. The small bridge over the flowing stream in the garden

4. The corridor with reception spaces

5. The vestibule in the warm and gentle light

3

4

6

7

6. The private open-air bath. In August, the blooming osmanthus blossom fills the room with fragrance.

7. The special guest room with wooden and ceramic bath tubs to let guests experience a different kind of bathing pleasure

8

8. The guest room in Japanese style with the exclusive open-air bath pool

9. The guest room combining the unique modern and traditional design style

10. The bed in the guest room

9

10

1

Nishiizu Toi Onsen Hotel Miyabi

Location: 241 Nishiizu Toi, Izu, Shizuoka Prefecture, 410 - 3301, Japan

Spa Name: Nishiizu Toi Onsen

Area: 4,890m²

Quantity of Guest Room: 17 with an accomodation capacity of 90 persons

Quantity of Spa Facilities: 4

Other Facilities: private open-air bath

Nestled in western Izu Peninsula, Nishiizu Toi Onsen Hotel was built with the advantage of the nearby Toi Gold Mine, a well-known scenic spot. Facing the White Sand Beach formed by the scouring waves in Suruga Bay, the hotel stands next to the cliff "Koyibito Misaki", famous for the hanging Love Clock. Guests can listen to the vivid rhythm of the waves in all the guestrooms that designed in modern Japanese style. In the setting sunlight, the combination of the golden sky and the sea looks as glare as an oil painting.

Being observed in the distance, the black granite and the red granite add radiance and beauty to each other. Guests can admire the stunning night scene of the small coastal town. They can also taste the banquet cuisine cooked with the seafood from Izu Peninsula, which has won the most public praise. The staff from South Korea and China can provide all-round services.

1. The facade of the Japanese spa hotel

2. The vestibule and the entrance

3. The exclusive open-air stone bath pool in the guest room, installed on 16-square-metre terrace

4

4. The ocean-view open-air pool

5. The guest room with the high-grade cypress bath, where you can enjoy the stunning scene of the sky and the broad Toi sea

6. Teahouse

7

8

9

7. Standard ocean-view guest room in Japanese style, approx.16 square metres (about 10 tatami mats), together with the wide corridor

8. The guest room with the open-air bath pool

9. The after-bath lounge

Toi Hotel Sankaitei

Location: 324 Nishiizu Toi, Izu, Shizuoka Prefecture, 410 - 3301, Japan

Spa Name: Izu Toi Onsen

Area: 1,430.89 m^2

Quantity of Guest Room: 40

Quantity of Spa Bath: 7

Other Facilities: private open-air bath, chartered spa

Located in western Izu Peninsula, Toi Hotel Sankaitei boasts the ideal location of famous scenic spots commanding a panoramic view of the gloriours scenenry of Toi in sunset glow. Guests can listen to the vivid tempo and melody of tide and spray and enjoy the stunning view of the setting sun while lying in the observatory open-air bath pool. The great flavour and interests of nature make guests intoxicated in endless enjoyment.

There are 21 guest rooms with exclusive open-air bath pools, and all are made of high-grade cypress. The modern Japanese style is fully demonstrated by the water-cycled natural spa and elegant and cosy guest rooms.

The observatory chartered open-air bath pool named "Yakata Takarabune" was made with the technology of the ship constructor. There are seven different kinds of spas such as the outdoor bath in the garden, the observatory open-air bath (Mabu Hot Spring), which are all available to guests.

Guests can leisurely enjoy fresh marine fish from the Toi Sea and vegetables prepared for breakfast and dinner in the guest rooms.

1. The rooftop open-air spa "Mabu Hot Spring" – exclusive for men

2. The lobby

3. The high-grade-cypress-made open-air bath pool in the shape of a wine goblet

4. All guest rooms in the new building "Ajisaitei" are equipped with open-air bath pool

5

5. The observatory open-air bath pool "Yakata Takarabune", built with exquisite workmanship. It is so pleased to overlook Suruga Bay while bathing in it.

3

4

1

Ochiairou Murakami

Location: 1887-1 Yujima, Izu, Shizuoka Prefecture, 410-3206, Japan

Spa Name: Izu Yujima Onsen

Quantity of Guest Room: 15

Quantity of Spa Bath: 4

Other Facilities: private open-air spa, rentable spa, foot spa

As a perfect example of incorporating Japanese and Western building style, Ochiairou Murakami has been written in National Cultural Heritage lists. It is a rare traditional wooden hotel. In Meiji 14 (1881 AD), Yamaoka Tesshū (1836-88AD), the Warrior, suggested renaming the hotel as Ochiairou, when he overlooked Kano River, the intersection of Hontani River and Neko River, and then it was known as "Ochiairou". Since the beginning of Meiji period, numerous literators have stayed at the onsen ryokan during their trips. The vestibule and the annexe named "Minuntei" were added continuously from Showa 8 to Showa 12 (1933-1938 AD). In the Japanese traditional academy-style guest rooms with antique beauty, the niche is installed next to the curio box shelf and the partition board door, which were both made with the mosaic craft, the same technique used in the design of the window lattice. They were both handmade by carpenters without using any iron nails or any adhesive, demonstrating the amazing craftsmanship.

Guest rooms can be classified into two categories: the ones facing the garden and the ones in the face of the river, which are heated by wood fire in winter and cooled by fresh air and clear stream gushing from Mount Amagi in summer, making guests fully relaxed in mind and body.

1. Ochiairou Murakami, surrounded by sakura in early spring

2. The front vestibule of the onsen ryokan in the ancient fine wooden structure, which was listed as the National Cultural Heritage

3. The chartered spa, in which you can admire the murmuring stream and river, breathe the fresh air and enjoy the cosy sunshine

4. The open-air bath pool, named "Tengu no Yu", comprising the stone bath pool and the brook-front bath pool

5. The façade

3

4

6. The Japanese banquet hall, adorned with delicate red sandalwood carving, simple and mellow

7. The reading room

8. The guest room named "Tsubaki" with Ashiyu (foot bath), where you can have a foot spa while observing the beautiful Kano River

7

8

9

9. The luxury guest room "Koubai" in the annexe "Minuntei"

10. Bedroom

1

Hotel Izukyu

Location: 2732 – 7 Shirahama, Shimoda, Shizuoka Prefecture, 415 – 8512, Japan

Area: 3,600 m^2

Capacity: 416 persons

Quantity of Spa Facilities: 4

Quantity of Guest Room: 117

Sited in the south of Izu Pennisula, Hotel Izukyu was built facing the snow-like Shirahama Coast, one of the eight wonderful scenes of Izu, which can be seen from both the reception hall and the guest rooms. Shirahama Onsen is unique in that it was excavated from its own properties, comprising two hot springs: Ryujin Onsen and Rendaiji Onsen, with their respective water quality and function; the former one has the special efficacy in treating arteriosclerosis, dermatosis and helps recovering from diseases, whereas the latter is exceptional in its function for relieving neurodynia, myalgia and arthralgia. The Department of General Affairs and the Marketing Department of the hotel were nominated as one of the "One Hundred Top Japanese Hotels" in the year of 2010.

HOTEL
IZUKYU

1. Night view. It offers you a totally different feeling to walk and play leisurely in the courtyard with lights everywhere.

2. The façade – the outdoor swimming pool in front of the hotel, where you can enjoy yourself swimming, while admiring the blue sky, the blue sea and Shirahama Coast

3-4. The open-air spa named "Banza Furo" with the spring resource from Ryujin Onsen, having the special efficacy in treating arteriosclerosis, dermatosis and helping recovering from diseases

5

5. The indoor spa bath – the clean and spacious bathing pool with the spring resource from Rendaiji Onsen, having the special efficacy in relieving neurodynia, myalgia and arthralgia and the function of bubble massage

3

4

6. The indoor spa bath – the clean and spacious bathing pool with the spring from Rendaiji Onsen, having the special efficacy in relieving neurodynia, myalgia and arthralgia

7. The reception room in the hall, bright and transparent, warm and cosy

8. The garden restaurant named "Kagayaki" offering buffet breakfast

7

8

9

10

11

9. The Japanese-style guest room

10. The luxury suite with the best location commanding a panoramic view of the picturesque view of the spacious sea, the snow-like Shirahama Coast at all seasons

11. The European-style guest room with simple but grand arrangement

1

Hoshinoya Karuizawa

Location: Hoshino, Karuizawa-machi, Nagano 389-0194, Japan

Spa Name: Hoshino Onsen

Area: 42,055 m²

Quantity of Guest Room: 77

Quantity of Spa Facilities: 2

"What would our life and the surrounding scenery be like if we reserve Japanese traditions while keep moving to modernization?" Hoshinoya Karuizawa has created another world of Japan under this ideal, which gave birth to the beautiful sights of "Countryside in the Valley".

All the guestrooms in Hoshinoya Karuizawa were built as single houses, thus a village was formed by the lanes connecting the houses. Those houses are now dotted along the creek, which runs through a small valley with the lush forests. In front of Mount Asama, Karuizawa is among the top few summer resorts in Japan. With cool climate in summer, Karuizuwa is located on the 1000-metre-high plateau area, where the Emperor met his lifetime mate by chance. In accordance with the different locations and construction procedures, the guestrooms here can be classified into Mizunami (the riverside villa), Yamaroji (the hillside villa) and Niwaroji (the garden villa). As an original Japanese holiday resort hotel showcasing the culture of Japan, Hoshinoya Karuizawa has been used to convey the Japanese culture to the world. Focusing on offering guests the chance of experiencing the great flavour and interest of Japanese hotel and the world top-class service with the value of protecting the environment and constituting a sound ecosystem, Hoshinoya Karuizawa endows guests with the superior Japanese service abreast of the times.

1. The overview of the village in summer

2. The panoramic view of the resort in the setting sun. Focusing on the theme of the resort hotel with the elements of Japanese villages, Hoshinoya Karuizawa is a typical sustainable hotel with a resource self-sufficiency rate of about 70%

3. The Meditation Bath – the meditative space to soothe and relax the soul, comprising Hikari-no-heya with bright light and the dark "Yami-no-heya" with the drifting faint sound

4. The interior of the Hoshinoya spa, providing the traditional Japanese Shiatsu massage, the oil treatment, to the original Reiki massage

5. The panoramic view of Tombo-no-yu

3

4

6. The exclusive spa room in Hoshinoya Karuizawa

7. The full view of the Japanese cuisine "Kasuke" cooked with the typical Japanese cooking ideas of "Five Flavours, Five Methods and Five Senses", the healthy Japanese courses that embrace tradition and feature the local delicacies and fresh ingredients from Karuizawa

8

9

8. The living room of the hillside house, which were built as single isolated villas leaning against the mountains; the room on the tall platform facing the birds and the forests

9. The living room in the garden house; the self-contained room within the bardian garden

10. The overview of the guest room on the hillside; spacious room with complete facilities

1

Hotel Hananoi

Location: 399 – 1 Kanznjicho, West District, Hamamatsu, Shizuoka Prefecture, 431-1209, Japan

Spa Name: Kanznjicho Onsen

Area: 2,775 m^2

Quantity of Guest Room: 14

Quantity of Spa Bath: 4

Other Facilities: private open-air bath, rentable bathroom

Hotel Hananoi enjoys the ideal location on the fields of fortune of Kanznjicho, which was firstly built in 810 AD, as early as 1,200 years ago. Kanznjicho Onsen was the great work by the designer who had successfully designed Hoshinoya Karuizawa and Izumi Hoshimo Hotel. With the central concept of harmony between the colours of gold and cyan-blue, and the unity of Japanese and Western styles, the interior design of high-class Liukiuu tatami in the gentle candle light, leads tourists immediately to a tranquil and cosy world.

Since its opening in 1958 (Shouwa 33), Kanznjicho Onsen has been widely used in that the appropriate temperature of salt solution has significant curative effect to neuralgia and rheumatalgia. Kanznjicho Onsen incorporates Koto no yu, the open-air spa, in which guests can feel the pleasant cool breeze, and Hananoyu including a large number of indoor spas such as the ones with massage bathtubs and saunas. The open outdoor spa and meditation spa, which are exclusive to men and women at different time intervals, offer guests differed spa experiences.

The guestrooms are located in the space from the fourth to the sixth floor all with a panoramic view of the Hamanako Lake, comprising the double-bed room with the cyclic annular floor, presidential room, Hananoi modern room with Liukiuu tatami, Hananoi premiere modern room, suite room with outdoor bath and the room for the disabled.

2

3

1. The atrium, the living environment design with the background of the natural environment, with the central design elements of "Universal Design"

2. The interior of the open-air spa "Koto no yu", the bath made of high-grade cypress

3. The exterior of the open-air spa "Koto no yu", where you feel sank in the tranquility with the breeze of Hamanako Lake passing by

4. The Japanese guest room incorporating the Western style – the interior space features the high-grade Liukiuu tatami, with the central idea of the harmony and unity between the colours of gold and cyan-blue and the combination of Japanese and Western style

5. The exclusive indoor bath made from superior cypress

6

6. The façade of the hotel

4

5

1

IDUMISOU

Location: 2 – 21 Okahiro-cho, Ito-city, Shizuoka Prefecture, 414-0016, Japan

Spa Name: Ito Onsen

Area: 5,264 m²

Number of Guest Room: 34

Spa Facilities: private open-air bath, chartered bath, foot spa

IDUMISOU lies in Izu Peninsula on the south of Tokyo. Ito spa comprises more than 750 hot springs with such an abundant stream volume that it can spout over 32,000 litre spring water per minute, which makes it one of the top famous spa resorts in Japan. With the concept of "Paradise with Unique Tranquility", IDUMISOU spa hotel boasts not only various spas indoor and outdoor, but also spas for family use and the foot spa, making guests feel at home.

Founded in 1912, IDUMISOU is available to guests all year round. From the spa bath and the open-air bath made of ancient cypress to the graceful 6,600 square metres' Japanese gardens in different styles, and even the fresh flowers eager to bloom all seasons, whose beautiful images are reflected in the spring water with vertical flow as well as the cosy and amiable natural oxygen bar, all these make guests feel so cheerful in mind and body that they forget all fatigue. They can also enjoy the seafood cuisine of Izu.

1. Founded in 1912, IDUMISOU spa hotel is designed with the concept of "Paradise with Unique Tranquility".

2. The night scene of the swimming pool with hot water, which is available all year round, forming a delightful contrast finely with the Japanese garden

3. The open-air bath for women encapsulated by trees. The drinking water of the waterfall and the stone bath comes from the headspring.

4. The indoor bath for women where you can admire the courtyard with the open-air bath and feel the natural oxygen bar permeating with the water mist splashed from the waterfall

5. The 6,600-square-metre Japanese courtyard in which the flowers are eager to bloom all seasons

3

4

6. Night scene of the independent Bettei guest room circled by the beautiful courtyard

7. The exclusive open-air cypress bath pool

8. The Bettei guest room located in the two-storey building equipped with the half-open bath built from Ito stone and the open-air bath made of ancient cypress

7

8

9

10

9. The elegant guest room in Japanese style, in which you can smell the fragrance of cypress, the original building material of the indoor bathroom

10. The Japanese restaurant "Zuiun", against the background of the picturesque traditional Japanese garden

11. The Japanese-style guest room with study room, dressing room, porch and eaves gallery, each having its unique layout

1

ANGINE

Location: 5-12 Nagisa-cho, Ito, Shizuoka Prefecture, 414-0023, Japan

Spa Name: Ito Onsen

Area: 6,031 m²

Quantity of Guest Room: 38

Quantity of Spa Bath: 4

Other Facilities: indoor exclusive spa

Facing the sea in the beauteous Ito Peninsula, Hoshino ANGINE spa hotel was designed by Japanese star architect Rie Azuma. Combining the traditional and modern design style, the hotel offers private spaces far away from metropolis life, endowing them with spiritual tranquility. With the name "ANGINE", derived from the name of the adviser on foreign affairs for "Tokugawa Leyasu", British navigator "William Adams". It features the colourful space such as the modern ocean-view Japanese-style guest room, the guest room with private spa and typical Japanese courtyard, surrounded by the stunning attractions and entertainments, such as Jyogasaki Coast, Izo Park, the fireworks in memory of the navigator "William Adams", the beautiful flowers and scenery as well as the open-air spa bath and the indoor spa bath called "Skincare Hot Spring", a series of spaces which are available to guests all the time during their stay.

The spas here all have their unique water qualities such as the alkalescence one and the hypotonicity one. It is interesting that the different water qualities are particularly effective in skincare, alleviating neuralgia, rheumatism, arthralgia and paralysis motorica.

1. The façade of the spa hotel facing the sea with its unique shape

2. The open-air bath for women, whose different water qualities have different effects. It is so interesting to admire the stunning landscape in the Japanese courtyard.

3. The evening view of the Japanese-style guest room

4. The reading room on the way between the guest room and spa pool, where there are abundant books and picture albums about Ito

5. The 2,640-square-metre Japanese Courtyard with picturesque trees and flowers, making guests intoxicated in the harmonious atmosphere of gardens and buildings

3

4

6

7

8

6. The guest room "Harare" with open-air spa

7. The restaurant "G[illegible]sutan" provides all-private-room service, enjoying the delicacies in the peaceful and cosy environment

8. The guest room mixed Japanese and Western style with a view of Ito Peninsula

1

Horai

Location: 750 – 6 Mount Ito, Atami, Shizuoka Prefecture, 413 – 0002, Japan

Spa Name: Atami Onsen

Area: 4,900 m^2

Quantity of Guest Room: 16

Quantity of Spa Bath: 3

Located on Mount Ito, Atami which has a panoramic view of Sagami Bay, Horai is founded in Kaei 2 (1849 AD), the end of the Edo period, a famous hotel with a history of about 160 years. The name "Horai" refers to a place on the eastern sea, where an ageless immortal lived. The guests can experience the unique paradise-like space. Various seasonal cuisine are served here with the pure flavour of the ingredients. All the guest rooms are both in traditional Japanese aroma such as the Japanese-style guest room on a high platform, the one with a courtyard, creating the atmosphere of Japanese traditional culture, as well as the building with the large open-air spa in Eastern traditional building style. Located in Shizuoka Prefecture near Tokyo, it is surrounded by attractions including Izu Mount Shrine with the unique culture of Japan.

As one of the Three Great Ancient Onsens in Japan, Izu Onsen is called Holy Spa by the faith followers, as it is next to Izu Mount Shrine. The spring quality of the vitoriol spring is particularly effective in curing empyrosis and incise lesion.

There are two open-air spas in Horai, "Hashiri-yu", which means running hot water and "Kogoi-no-yu", which is designed by Kengo Kuma, a famous architect.

1. The guest room with the tranquil Japanese style, where the attractive views inside and outside create different feelings

2. The façade of the superior Japanese spa hotel located in the peaceful Izu Mount

3. The open-air spa "Hashiri-Yu"

4. Kogoi-No-Yu designed by Kengo Kuma Architects

5. The lobby, in which the considerate services with Japanese cultural spirits attracts guests all over the world

3

4

6. The teahouse-like guest room permeated with the flavour of the traditional culture of Japan

7. One of the guest rooms in the traditional Japanese style

8. The luxury Japanese-style guest room decorated with ornaments implying the spirits of Horai

8

1

Kishoan

Location: 1 – 31 – 1, Matsumoto City, Nagano Prefecture, 390 – 0303, Japan

Spa Name: Asama Onsen

Area: 3,464 m²

Quantity of Guest Room: 26

Quantity of Spa Bath: 13

Other Facilities: private open-air spa

Located in eastern Matsumoto City in central Nagano, Kishoan was designed by famous modern architect Takao Habuka & S.E.N Architects Associates. The hot springs in Kishoan are called "Taka No Yu" and the well-known "Zenkouji Onsen", which incorporate 82 kinds of spring stream, providing different spa experiences. All the guest rooms and the spas enjoy the individual design with the cob wall and the Japanese paper as the keynote, taking the open-air spa "Kiten" as an example, whose natural wooden material expresses a sense of beauty, matched with round windows. Whether the entrance hall or the corridor or even the guest rooms, are designed with unique themes, whilst the guest rooms, moreover, seem quietly elegant in the embellished light, featuring the brisk colour and tone.

Combining the elegant façade and the contemporary design, Hoshino Kishoan Spa endows the whole hotel with a grand style. Kishoan Onsen is exclusive to men and women at different time intervals in the morning and in the evening. The simple alkaline water of the 13 characteristic spas including the radiant heated bath and the open-air spa, has significant effects to neuralgia, gastroenterology, gynecological diseases, dermatitis and diabetes mellitus.

Guests can taste different Shinshu Kaiseki, the local food of Shinshu with the highest-grade wine, changed with seasons.

1. The waterfall fountain in the patio

2. The façade of the spa resort hotel; the traditional elements designed in modern style by the famous Takao Habuka & S.E.N Architects Associates

3. The indoor spa named "Kiten", made with the rare natural wood – an indoor bath with extreme openness, produced by the patio stretching out to the forum

4

4. The detail of the indoor communal spa named "Kiten", producing a poetic elegance with the ornament of the lighting

5

5. The open-air spa named "Kiten", in which the design of the round window expresses a kind of Japanese beauty

6. The open-air bath in the guestroom, made of natural black granite

7. The corridor to the guestroom, and each part was designed with its unique artistic theme by the designer

6

7

8. The panoramic view of the guestroom with open-air spa

9. The guestroom with open-air spa, in which the gentle light and the spring scenery of the garden can be seen through the lenient windows on the terrace

10. The guestroom with open-air spa

9

10

1

Sun Hatoya Hotel

Location: 572 – 12, Yukawa, Ito-City, Shizuoka Prefecture, 414 – 0002, Japan

Spa Name: Ito Onsen

Area: 16,141 m²

Quantity of Guest Room: 191

Quantity of Spa Bath: 8

The coastal location of Sun Hatoya in central Izu Peninsula commands a panoramic view of the stunning seascape for each room. In the submarine hot spring, the only one in Japan, guests can enjoy the spa bath. With the central theme of "Ancient Monuments–Submarine Adventure", the indoor swimming-wear-required hot spring zone includes Exploration Zone, Mystery Fall Zone, Stream Swimming Pool Zone and Children's Swimming Pool Zone, among which you can admire the roaming fish while bathing in Fish Bathing Pool. Being a unique scenery line of the hotel, the aquarium-like spa endows guests with the pleasant sensation in enjoying the cosy spa and the underwater world. The spa bath with historical remains and the outdoor swimming pool nearby are bathing places where guests need to wear their swimming wears. The indoor spa bath with historical remains is available in all seasons. The name of the submarine spa derives from the natural flow gushed out of the 1,000-metre-deep submarine hot spring, which is rarely seen in Japan and the spas in all rooms come from the same spring resource .

Monthly different dishes are served here, beside performance in the banquet hall with a capacity of 1,000 persons. There are dancing hall with a capacity of 800 people, the game rooms and the karaoke.

1. The night scene of the appearance of the hotel standing on Ito coast

2. The submarine spa

3. The submarine spa

4. The ocean-view restaurant named "Daigyouen", which features the fresh seafood cuisine

5

5. The layout of the submarine spa

3

4

6

7

6. The banquet hall, enjoy daily night performances by the well-known troupe with actors from across the world. There are 626 seats on the ground floor and 202 on the first floor.

7. The banquet hall with performance stage

8. The banquet hall with performance stage

Hotel Hatoya

Location: 1391 Oka, Ito, Shizuoka Prefecture, 414 - 0055, Japan

Spa Name: Ito Onsen

Area: 11,379 m²

Quantity of Guest Room: 162

Quantity of Bath: 2

Located in Oka, Ito Peninsula, Hotel Hatoya and Sun Hatoya are two hotels of the same brand. The most distinguishing feature of the hotel is that guests here can play the submarine adventure game using the facilities in the submarine spa of Sun Hatoya Hotel, the chain hotel, enjoying the great pleasure in the spa and the underwater world just like the guests in Sun Hatoya Hotel.

The five large spa pools with local natural hot spring are highly praised by spa experts for its appropriate water temperature for human body and the skin care. The guest can not only enjoy the spa bath, but also oversee the stunning scene of Ito in the guestrooms permeated with elegant atmosphere. It is really a very good choice for holiday.

There are over 70 kinds of choices including seafood and local food for buffet dinner.

1. The façade

2. The indoor spa pool for women

3. The indoor spa pool for women

4. The indoor cypress-made bath pool

5. The reception hall

3

4

6. The indoor large communal bath for men

7. The meeting room named "Kuzyu" with an area of 145 square metres and a capacity of 60 persons

8. The meeting room named "Orange" with an area of 111 square metres and a capacity of 90 persons

9

9. The banquet hall with performance stage, with an area of 850 square metres and a capacity of 510 persons on the ground floor and 152 persons on the first floor

10. The entertainment room with table-tennis

11. The Japanese-style guestroom

10

11

1

Sora Togetsusou Kinryu

Location: 3455 Shuizenji, Izu-shi, Shizuoka Prefecture, 410-2416, Japan

Spa Name: Shuizenji Onsen

Area: 49,500 m^2

Quantity of Guest Room: 29

Quantity of Spa Bath: 4 indoor spas, 4 outdoor spas

Other Facilities: private open-air spa, rentable outdoor spa

Shuizenji Onsen Zone is a spa street along Katsuragawa. It is said that the hot spring was made by the eminent monk "Kobo Daishi" with its withered stick in order to cure the old mother's sickness whose son work hard all day looking after her, which made the monk deeply moved. The original hot spring is the Shuizenji Onsen today. It was in this advantaged location that the Japanese spa hotel with the modern concept was designed. Sora Togetsusou Kigru boasts a private courtyard with an area of 49,500m^2, encompassing 45 to 49 temples of the nearby tourist attraction " Keikoku 88".

Sora Togetsusou Kinryu focused on its concept with the use of light, whose transparency creates a unique space feeling. The most outstanding spa is the only-one "Lights Open-Air Bath" in Japan designed by the famous interior designer, Tsujimura Hisanobu. The unique spa was highlighted in almost all magazines in Japan and had won the Excellent Award in the NASHOP Lighting Awards. Bathing in the lighted-glass-made pool seems like travelling in the universe.

The unique design can also be found in the private dinning room "Kumo-no-niwa", whose walls are all embedded with spotlights, making guests feel like dinning in a lightened box. However, the food in this fashionable restaurant are exquisite traditional Kaiseki (the advanced Japanese feast). The ideal location on the hillside of Mount Shuizenji enables guests to admire the stunning sceneries around while enjoying the cuisine.

1. The façade of restaurant "Kumo-no-niwa", locating on the hillside of Mount Shuizenji enables guests to admire the stunning sceneries around while enjoying the cuisine

2. The garden in autumn – the traditional Japanese garden with an area of 49,500 square metres

3. The vestibule in summer

4. The pathway in the bamboo forest

5. The façade of the hotel, surrounded by mountains; the sunlight transmitted through the woods leads guests to the paradise

3

4

6

7

8

6. The surroundings of "Dokko No Yu"
7. The open-air spa made of natural stone
8. The vestibule in autumn

9

9. The interior space of "Open-Air Spa of Sunset" which means admiring the beautiful setting sun while bathing

10. The exterior space of "Open-Air Spa of Sunset"

11. "Open-Air Bath of Lights" all made of light boxes, a lightened open-air spa at night

10

11

12

12. One of the guest rooms facing the mountains and the fields with red leaves, comprising a guest room with an area of 20 square metres, 9.9-square-metre corridor and the indoor spa

13. One of the guest rooms facing the mountains and the fields with green trees, comprising a guest room with an area of 20 square metres long and 9.9-square-metere corridor and the indoor spa

14. The corridor of the restaurant "Kumo-no-niwa" whose walls are all embedded with spotlights

13

14

Atami Sakuraya Ryokan

Location: 9 – 11 Higashikaigancho, Atami-shi, Shizuoka Prefecture, 413-0012, Japan

Spa Name: Atami Onsen

Area: approx. 1,983 m^2

Quantity of Guest Room: 21

Quantity of Spa: 4

It is only five minutes walk to Atami Sakuraya Ryokan from Atami Railway Station and three minutes walk from the Atami Beach. Hided in the forests with the surrounding green trees in the central area of Atami, it enjoys the ideal location in the hinterland, the scenic spot of Atami where you can see the first plum blossom and the Atami onsen had won praise from the first general Tokugawa Ieyasu.

With the basic service concept of "the only lucky chance in life", the hotel makes guests fully relaxed here. The open-air spas comprise the superior cypress bath and the stone bath made of the natural Izu rock. Various spa baths are available to men and women at different time intervals.

The guest rooms are in two types: "Touzankaku" (Ocean Front Guest Rooms) and "Sihoukaku" which are in various styles such as the Japanese style, the Japanese and Western style and the double deck. All guest rooms are equipped with spa baths with their own characteristics and elegant tastes. The most outstanding one is the highly-praised Japanese and western guestroom with a large bed and the Kotatsu on the first floor of Touzankaku, in which guests can have a panoramic view of the surrounding mountains and rivers through the open window.

The cuisine features the luxurious feast with seasonal seafood from Suruga Bay, which can be enjoyed in the guest rooms.

2

3

1. The façade of the quiet and beautiful hotel

2. The "Kaisei No Yu" with baths of the horizontal type

3. The guest room equipped with the exclusive open-air bath pool, connected with the courtyard

4. The spa pool named "Kaisei no Yu"

5. The spa pool named "Tensei no Yu" with sauna

6

6. The hall in ancient style

4
5

7. The guest room

8. The standard guest room with overview of Sagami Bay through the large window

9. The guest room of mixed Japanese and European style

8

9

1

Yagyu-No-Sho

Location: 1116-6, Shuzenji, Izu-shi, Shizuoka, 410-2416, Japan

Spa Name: Shuzenji Onsen

Area: 10,000 m^2

Quantity of Guest Room: 15

Quantity of Spa Bath: 4

Yagyu-No-Sho is a luxurious high-end traditional hotel in the well-known Shuzenji Onsen area. Built in 1970 as the annexe of the high-class Tokyo Ryotei "Yagyu-no-Sho", it was designed in the form of the bamboo court, creating a natural sense of beauty. The main building was built in the traditional style. There are 15 Japanese guest rooms and 2 independent apartments. The annexe, the independent guest rooms named "Matsu-no-o" and "Ume-no-o", are perfectly matched with the natural environment such as green bamboos, the mountain forest, the pool, the light and shadow. All the space from the vestibule to the guest room is permeated with the sense of Japanese Zen. Guest rooms were designed in above ten Japanese styles such as the one in the style of the academy of science, the teahouse style and the farmhouse style, implying perfect combination of the traditional Japanese culture, modern culture and humanity.

The hypotonic low alkaline hot spring (PH8.7) has the efficacy of softening the cuticle, and 65mg moisturising elements per kilogramme in the water make it "Spring of Skin Care".

In the original intention of making guests taste the gourmet in the natural environment of Ryotei, the owner built the private hot spring Ryotei. With 30-year-cooking experience, the head chef "Sibayama Takashi" is good at cooking Izu local ingredients such as Izu beef, Izu tricholoma matsutake and Ise lobster in different methods, offering guests various kinds of delicious food.

2

1. The vestibule in autumn

2. The façade of the top exquisite Ryotei spa hotel located in the deep tranquil area of Shuzenji

3. The exterior bath pool of the open-air spa "Musashi-no-yu"

4. The vestibule in summer, built with Tamajyari

5. The independent guest room in the annexe named Matsuo

6. The exclusive bath pool in the guest room "Yuuzuki"

7. The open-air bath "Ichiju"

8. The indoor bath pool of the open-air spa "Musashi-no-yu"

9. The ceramic bath pool of "Fish Pavilion"

8
9

10. The guest room "Yuuzuki"

11. The flower arrangement – the interior decoration in autumn

12. The Japanese guest room "Hatsukari", with semi-open spa pool

11

12

1

ASABA Ryokan

Location: 3450 – 1, Shuzenji, Izu-shi, Shizuoka Prefecture, Japan

Spa Name: Shuzenji Onsen

Quantity of Guest Room: 17

Capacity: 50 persons

Quantity of Spa Bath: 3

Other Facilities: chartered spa 2

Located in Monzenmachi, Shuzenji, Izu-shi, Shizuoka Prefecture, ASABA Ryokan was found in 1489 with a history of more than 520 years, when the ancestor Asaba Yakurouyukitada, who was the general following Chan master Ryukeihansho, the founder of the mountain, came to guard a temple. It was those ancestors who created the oldest spa hotel in Shuzenji Temple. At the end of Meiji, under the protection of Asaba, the seventh owner of the hotel, Yasuemon removed the Gekkeiden Noh Stage here from Fukagawa Tommiokahachimangu, which made ASABA Ryokan a well-known high-ranking spa hotel with Noh performance in Japan. With a garden area of 1,980 square metres, ASABA Ryokan is surrounded by green hills and blue water. Attracted by the spa water quality and abundant spring flow, a large number of guests come here to see Noh and Munchausen, performed here numerous times in a year. Surrounded by the bamboo forest, the interior decoration and the exterior building are both in the traditional Japanese style, overlooking the large and broad pond. The open-air spa, hidden in the lush green bamboo forest, with the birds' twitter and fragrance of flowers, the whirling and murmuring sound of the bamboo forest and the fresh air. Moreover, there are also Koya-Maki Baths, Baths for Ladies, Baths for Gentlemen and Family Baths.

1. The panoramic view of the famous spa hotel with a long history of several hundred years

2. The panoramic night scene of the hotel

3. The vestibule

4. The Gekkeiden Noh Stage, the Noh drama stage built with authentic pine

5. The Gekkeiden Noh Stage, a Noh drama theatre opposite the hotel, removed from Fukagawa Tomioka Hachimangu Shrine, Tokyo

6. The outdoor pool Koyamaki-wood bath

7. The artistic lounge & salon

6

7

8. The spa for ladies
9. The guest room
10. The guest room

9

10

HANAFUBUKI Ryokan

Location: 1041 Yawata, Ito-shi, Shizuoka Prefecture, 413-0232, Japan

Spa Name: Izukogen Spa

Area: approx. 13,000 m^2

Capacity: 45 persons

Quantity of Guest Room: 17

Quantity of Spa Facilities: 7

Located in Yawata, Ito-shi, Shizuoka Prefecture along the Fuji Mount, Hakone and the Kinosaki coastline of Izu Natioanl Park, HANAFUBUKI Ryokan was designed with the concept of "Onsen Forest", while the most outstanding design was the spa in the jungle. When entering, guests are led by the gate to a green world of a large area of forest and the open-air spa also surrounded by jungle. The spas are made of natural wood such as cypress and Kuromoji. Taking Kuromoji-Yu as an example, it was made of the local tree called Kuromoji, which produces a light smell of aroma when sank in the hot spring, thus becoming guests' favourite. Whether in the indoor or the outdoor spa, guests can breathe the fresh air from the forest and are set in a mood surpassing that of the immortals in the quiet courtyard with the moss floor, the bug buzz and the birds' song. They can simply go to any of the seven Onsen, get in, lock the entrance, and enjoy Onsen bathing freely, with families or with friends. All onsens here are available 24 hours.

HANAFUBUKI Ryokan features the Kaiseki cuisine with "Sakura" theme favoured by tourists, which can offer guests the most original local gourmet of Izu Plateau.

The most popular HANAFUBUKI breakfast menu hasn't been changed for three years and has won many awards.

1. The vestibule entrance "Gate of the Forest", the beginning of the cosy holiday

2. The independent guest room of Hakuo Villa hidden in the forest

3. Kuromoji-Yu spa including the indoor and the outdoor ones made from the local tree called Kuromoji, which produces a light smell of aroma when sank in the hot spring

4. The half-open-air spa made from Izu stone and cypress, with fresh breeze from the forest coming through the opened window

5. The night scene of the hotel

3

4

6

6. The wooden outdoor balcony of Hakuo Villa
7. The entrance of Hina-No-Yu
8. Oribe-Yu decorated with Oribe-Yaki

7

8

9. Shino-No-Yu decorated with Shino-Yaki

10. Kuromoji-Yu spa interior

11. The bath tub of Hina-No-Yu made from the clean Izu stone and cypress

10

11

12

12. Hina-No-Yu Spa built in 2006, where you can enjoy the simple and beautiful atmosphere far away from the metropolis

13. The spacious and tranquil interior space of Hakuo Villa

14. The Japanese conversation room with a capacity of 4 to 5 people

15. The guest room, where you can catch sight of the garden on the balcony

16. The small Japanese guest room of Hushi Villa in the teahouse style

15

16

1

Isawa View Hotel

Location: Nakajima 1607, Isawa-cho, Fuefuki City, Yamanashi Prefecture, 406-0024, Japan

Spa Name: Isawa Onsen

Area: 4,750 m^2

Quantity of Guest Room: 50

Quantity of Spa Bath: 4

Other Facilities: private open-air spa, chartered spa

It takes only one and a half hour from Tokyo to Isawa View Hotel by trolley bus, which is located in Kawanakajima, Isawa-cho, Fuefuki City, Yamanashi Prefecture. Isawa Onsen Town is the largest hot springs in Yamanashi Prefecture. One kilometre away is the Sakuragi standing in a line on each side of the river, and then the hotel can be seen at the end of the "Sakuragi Onsen Street". With elegant facilities, the hotel has long been pursuing the refined Japanese sensibility and sincerity. The guest rooms are in pure Japanese style and are created to provide a calm ambience, in which you can understand the spirit of the Japanese culture and time flowing slowly in harmony. Mt.Fuji can be viewed from the south-oriented rooms on a fine day. In the open-air spas blessed with unique amorous feelings, the name "Keiryu" endows the gentlmen's spa pool with more calmness and "Seiryu" brings more rustic atmosphere to ladies' spa pool. The guests can warm their bodies to the core while feeling the breezes of the seasons in the clear air of the rotenburo of which the hotel is very proud.

The stature of Ikkyu san, one of the most famous three monks in Japanese history, half lying down at the entrance, welcomes guests from across the world. While entering the hall, guests will see the design with the theme of "Interweaving Light and Water" immediately. Time seems stop while staying with the swimming fish silently.

The experienced chef cooks Kaiseki Ryori food with abundant seasonal ingredients of Yamanashi.

石和 びゅーほてる

1. The façade detail

2. The façade of the hotel

3. The fish pond next to the hall

4. The gentlmen's open-air spa

5. The vestibule and the statue of Ikkyu san, greeting guests from across the world

6. The hall with the remarkable electrolier lamp in the shape of a gamp and the adjacent pond full of fancy carps

3

4

7

8

7. Gentlmen's spa, "Keiryu", the spacious space that boasts abundant hot water and a calm atmosphere, equipped with massage bathtubs and bubble bathtubs

8. Ladies' spa, "Seiryu", with open space perfect for relaxing

9. The open-air spa where you can enjoy the natural scenery

10

11

10. Fish pond

11. The teahouse

12. The spacious and calm guest room in pure Japanese style, making guests feel at ease when resting here

1

Hotel Hana-Isawa

Location: Matsumoto 1409, Isawa-cho, Fuefuki City, Yamanashi Prefecture, 406-0021, Japan

Spa Name: Isawa Onsen

Area: 9,550 m²

Quantity of Guest Room: 69

Quantity of Spa Bath: 5

Other Facilities: private open-air spa, chartered spa

It only takes five minutes to the Hotel Hana-Isawa, located in Matsumoto, Isawa-cho, Fuefuki City, Yamanashi Prefecture by JR (Japanese Railway). With the concept of "enjoy your easy and cosy spa time", Hotel Hana-Isawa features overflowing onsen with a hot spring source coming from its properties, the natural flow with abundant hot water. There are two types of rotemburos: "Retemburo Hoshikuzu No Yu" and "Retemburo Gessho No Yu", with the different themes of gentle and strong style. The most popular onsen that continuously overflows from the bath tub is a proprietary onsen known for its soft and smooth properties. It has a refreshing effect to skin. The glass walls of the large public bath presents with a feeling of liberation and openness. Various choices of guest rooms are offered, such as Japanese-style rooms, Western and Japanese-style rooms and "Karei" Bungalow with Rotemburo, accompanying with guests to enjoy the luxury leisure time.

In Japan, the introduction of onsen is always coupled with that of the Japanese cuisine. With the local elements of Yamanashi Prefecture, Kaiseki Ryori is created by experienced chef. The traditional Japanese cuisine is brought in courses one by one, into which the chef has incorporated the careful choices of ingredients. The semi-private dinning room "Hanakomichi" has a high sense of privacy and provides a moment of elegance. The exquisite cuisine is made of seasonal ingredients. The cuisine contents and even the crockery are changed with seasons.

花いさわ

1. The entrance

2. The façade of the hotel, which re-opened after the renovation in 2002

3. The open-air spa "Rotemburo Gessho No Yu"

4. Spa "Afureide no Yu" with the onsen that continuously overflows from the bath tub, a proprietary onsen well-known for its very soft properties

5

5.Guest room "Karei" Bungalow with Rotemburo

3

4

6. The open-air spa "Rotemburo Hoshikuzu no Yu"

7. The private dinning room "Hana-Isawa", the restaurant with private rooms (for up to 4 persons) equipped with "hori-kotatsu" (low heated table with legroom built into the floor). Guests can spend a blissful moment savouring each of the dishes one by one

8. The dinning room "Hanakomichi" is semi-private dining room, equipped with "hori-kotatsu", which has a high sense of privacy and provides a moment of elegance

7

8

9. A warm and cosy Japanese-style room with an area of 16.5 square metres

10. "Karei" Bungalow with Rotemburo designed with a height of a patio, offering a feeling of leisure and openness

11. The private dinning room equipped with "hori-kotatsu"

10
11

Kasugai View Hotel

Location: Shizume 178, Kasugai-cho, Fuefuki-City, Yamanashi Prefecture, 406-0021, Japan

Spa Name: Isawa Onsen

Area: 10,367 m^2

Quantity of Guest Room: 71

Quantity of Spa Bath: 4

Other Facilities: private open-air spa, rentable spa

Nestled in Isawa Onsen in central Kofu Basin, Yamanashi Prefecture, Kasugai View Hotel features the statue of kind and friendly Ikkyu san, relaxing enviroment and delicious food. At the entrance of the hotel, the statue of the kind and friendly monk, Ikkyu san is welcoming guests from the world. Walking inside, the reception hall decorated with large pieces of glass with a height to the patio is full of gentle and warm sunlight. There are three Japanese and Western-style guest rooms among the 71 guest rooms with spacious and free interior space. Covering an area of 8 tatami mats to 12.5 tatami mats (13 square metres to 23 square metres), the Japanese guest rooms with typical Japanese elements and interest are all paved with Japanese tatami. The open-air spas boast alkaline simple hot spring with plentiful volume. You can enjoy bathing while admiring the pastoral scenery with rustic interest and grand openness.

The Fuefukigawa area in Kofu Basin, the location of Kasugai View Hotel, has long been crowned as "Fruit and Onsen Town", where grows a large area of peach trees and vineyards. It enjoys the largest output of peaches and grapes in Japan. In summer, tourists can take part in the self-help peach picking events, whilst grape picking festival in autumn.

Buffet dinner here provides crabs, freshly-baked beef, kebabs, etc. The cosy and tranquil Japanese dinning room provides more than 40 kinds of Japanese and Western food as well as the famous refined wine of Yamanashi Prefecture.

2

3

1. The façade

2. The reception hall decorated with large pieces of glass with a height to the patio in the hug of the gentle and warm sunlight

3. The hall

4. The bathing pool

5

5. The open-air spa, enjoy bathing while feeling the breezes of the seasons in the rotemburo, the pride of the hotel

6

6. The banquet hall with an area of 48 tatami mats (78 square metres), which can accommodate 48 persons

7. The dining room in which both breakfast and dinner are buffet-style

8. The Japanese-style guest room, which is recommended to those guests who wish to relax

9. The Western and Japanese-style guest room with two choices of 10-square-metre and 16.5-square-metre

10. The Western-style double-bed, economical room for business or couple trip

10

Southern Cross Resort Hotel

Location: 1006 Yoshida, Ito City, Shizuoka Prefecture, 414-0051, Japan

Spa Name: Ito Onsen

Area: 720,000 m²

Quantity of Guest Room: 55

Quantity of Spa Bath: 2

Other Facilities: private spa bath

Seated in Yoshida, Ito City, Shizuoka Prefecture, Southern Cross Resort Hotel is surrounded by charming sceneries and beautiful landscapes such as Mount Fuji on its north, the seven Izu Islands on the south, Sagami Bay on the east and Mount Amagi on the west. Covering a total area of 720,000 square metres, it is equipped with an 18-hole championship golf course and 6-hole golf course.

The onsen of spa in the Southern Cross Resort Hotel comes from a source within its own properties and there are also water floating activities designed in the swimming pool with hot spring. In spring, blooming flowers can be found everywhere in the hotel. Different kinds of flowers changed with seasons, decorating each and every corner of the golf course. Wandering in the golf course with the aroma of natural flowers and grass makes you a part of the whole nature.

Izu Peninsula is a scenic spot with the blessed mountains and sea. All ingredients are locally produced, including the fresh marine fish caught in the coastal waters. Guests are also provided with Guri tea from Izu and Wasabi from Amagi.

1. The façade
2. The façade of Southern Cross Resort Hotel
3. Night view of open-air spa
4. The swimming pool with warm water is available all year round

5. The view of Mount Fuji in the golf course

3

4

6

7

8

6 The club with the amenities such as the bar and the karaoke hall

7 The dining room serving Italian set meal and Japanese Kaisseki Ryori for dinner

8. The guest room mixed Japanese and Western style

9. The guest room for business use
10. The standard guest room
11. The Western-style guest room

10
11

Hotel Laforet Nasu

Location: 206-959, Yumoto, Nasu-machi, Nasu-gun, Tochigi Prefecture, Japan

Spa Name: New Nasu Spa

Area: 28,027 m^2

Quantity of Guest Room: 118

Quantity of Spa Bath: 4

Shiobara Onsen Town on the upstream of Houkigawa is just on the southwest of Nasu Highland. It is crownded as "Shiobara 11 Onsens" for the 11 onsens there. In autumn with red maple leaves, the surrounding area of the stream presents beautiful and colourful views such as the Momijidani suspension bridge with a total length of 320 metres at the entrance of the onsen town, the Kaiko suspension bridge along the sightseeing pedestrian street and the Kaiko waterfall, which are the ideal places commanding a view of the stunning scenery.

Hotel Laforet Nasu is located on Nasu Plateau, north of Tochigi Prefecture on the upstream of Naka River. The plateau area rolling up and down at the foot of Nasu Volcano is dotted with onsens such as Hakoneyumoto Onsen, Daimaru Onsen, which make up Nasu Onsen Town. Hotel Laforet Nasu is located on Nasu Plateau with stunning natural landscape in all seasons. Tourists can catch sight of beautiful scenery of continuous mountains of the grand Nasu Plateau, namely, the red maple leaves in autumn and the emerald green branches in spring, whether from the guestrooms or the bath area. The soft and smooth hot spring of the spa, in milky white, has the special efficacy for skincare. The hotel is highly proud of the Western-style cuisine cooked with natural ingredients and the traditional banquet cuisine.

The interior space is equipped with facilities such as conference room, banquet hall and arena. There are also a large number of surrounding recreational facilities such as the tennis court, golf court and ski resort and attractions of various kinds near Nasu Plateau such as Nasu Gallery, Nasu Zoo as well as Nikko Toshogu, the world heritage.

1. The façade of the hotel located on Nasu Plateau with the stunning natural landscape in all seasons

2. The night scene of the façade

3. The indoor large public bath with hot spring in milky white, where you can overlook Nasu Plateau out of the window

4. The conference room

5. The spacious hall

3

4

6. The dinning hall

7. The Japanese-style guest room with an area of 42.7 square metres

8. The interior space of the independent house with an area of 75.5 square metres, in which there is a spacious living room for group events

7

8

9

10

11

9. The guest room, mixing Japanese and Western style

10. The Western-style guest room in the main colour of brownish gold

11. The luxury guest room

1

Laforet Club Hotel Naka-Karuizawa

Location: 4339 Nagakura, Karuizawa-machi, Kitasaku-gun, Nagano, 389-0111, Japan

Spa Name: Karuizawa Shiotsubo Onsen

Quantity of Guest Room: 84

Quantity of Spa Bath: 4

It takes only one and a half hour by trolley bus from Tokyo to the famous Karuizawa Resort located in Kanto, Japan. The hotel buildings are surrounded by green trees, which make you feel like staying in a fictitious land of peace and happiness. It features double-bed rooms and an annexe which can accommodate 10 persons. The simple quality of the hot spring is particularly effective in curing neuralgia, digestive system disease and alleviating fatigue.

The cuisine prepared for guests includes authentic French Cuisine, roast meat, etc. There are also a large number of tourist attractions nearby such as old Karuizawa Ginza, Karuizawa Shopping Centre, Shiozawa Lake and the stunning scenery of red maples in Kumo ba Pond.

It is a hotel amidst the surrounding trees in the full-dodied Karuizawa style. Various facilities such as onsens, beauty salons and golf courses can be found here. Tourists can spend unforgettable leisure time here with the extreme elegant facilities from the tranquil and cosy guestrooms to the dinning room and the spa.The classic Karuizawa cuisine matches perfectly with the fresh and cool Karuizawa dinner. The local ingredients in fresh colours are cooked elaborately by the cooks. Tourists may feel satisfied with whether the entrée or the jardinière.

1. The façade of the hotel which enjoys full openness in the beautiful environment of blue sky and green grass

2. The façade of the independent annexe with adequate privacy in the embrace of the nature

3. The reception lobby made from marble, making guests feel comfortable

4. The vestibule

5. The streamlet in the garden of the hotel

3

4

6. The façade of the dinning hall
7. One corner of the open-air spa

8

8. The large spa bath with a river running outside the window just like a white ribbon

9. The luxury double guest room

10. The standard double guest room

9

10

Laforet Club Hotel Ito

Location: 2-3-1 Shishido, Ito City, Shizuoka Prefecture, 414－0004, Japan

Spa Name: Ito Onsen

Area: 3,800.47 m^2

Capacity: 360

Quantity of Guest Room: 84

Quantity of Spa Bath: 7

Other Facilities: rentable spa

It is only eight minutes' walk from Ito Station to Laforet Club Hotel Yitou, which locates in the east of Izu Peninsula, only 100 kilometres away from Tokyo. Located next to the Ito Orange Beach, it enjoys a tranquil environment and is very suitable for relaxing.

Simple but comfortable rooms are available with wireless network, which is convenient for searching information about the sightseeing facilities and scenic spots. There are so many tourist attractions nearby such as Jogasaki Beach, Izu Kogen, Sakura Town and Omuroyama.

The cuisine served is mainly seafood dishes, among which the marine fish are from the nearby Ito Port. The hot spas use the colourless and transparent simple alkaline spring water which has unique efficacy in curing neuralgia, muscle pain and alleviating fatigue, suitable for those tired guests after long-term travel.

1. The façade
2. The fountain in the atrium
3. The rentable spa for family

4. The wooden spa pool

3

5. The rockstone-made spa pool, named "Kenjin no Yu" has a long history

6. The Ball Jointed Doll show on "Hinamaturi" (The Daughter's Festival) on March 3rd

7. The hall

8. The dinning hall

9. The guest room, mixing Japanese and Western style

8

9

Zagyosoh

Location: 1741, Yawatano, Ito City, Shizuoka Prefecture, Japan

Spa Name: Ukiyama Hotspring Village

Area: 13,200 m^2

Quantity of Guest Room: 20

Quantity of Spa Bath: 4

Other Facilities: private open-air spa, rentable spa

Located in Ukiyama Hotspring Village, Ito City, Zagyosoh is a Japanese-style hotel full of the lasting appeal and aroma of the harbour city. It takes only two hours from Tokyo by trolley bus. Founded in 1968 with a covering area of 13,000 square metres, it boasts 20 elaborately decorated guest rooms. You can catch sight of the hundred-year-old peach trees, like the dotted stars in the sky, on the beautiful Kinosaki Coast, the waterfall outpouring from the mountains inside the natural garden formed by interweaved lava in thousands of postures, and the six spa facilities in different styles such as Teien-Roten Buro, Fuhketsu Roten Buro and Tenjyou Ocean Front Open-air Spa. The simple alkaline hot spring is so gentle and smooth that bring joyness of spa.

All guest rooms are in the typical Japanese style with the fragrance of the natural cypress, the Japanese aroma of tatami and the comfortable feeling of the natural gardens, which make guests fully intoxicated.

Japanese Kaiseki is served for dinner with the main ingredient of marine fish. Guests can not only taste the natural flavour by enjoying the elaborately cooked cuisine, but also feel the traditional Japanese hospitality.

1. The vestibule of Syoukintei, the independent guest room of the annexe

2. The vestibule

3. The sunset view

4 The open-air spa "Fuketsu"

5

5. The garden of the eastern building inside the typical Japanese-style hotel with natural gardens and interesting spa facilities on the 13,200-square-metre site

3

4

6. The interior garden of the guest room "Hatsune"

7. The open-air spa "Teien", the stone open-air bath in the green garden which makes your bath so close to nature

8. The chartered open-air spa commanding a panoramic view of the beautiful landscape of Sagami Bay and Izu Oshima

8

9

9. The verandah of Syoukintei, the independent guest room of the annexe

10. The indoor spa "Ukibune", made of high-grade cypress, in which you can admire the peach trees

11. Terrace stretching out to the garden area

10

12

13

14

12. The large and spacious banquet hall equipped with a stage

13. The guest room of Syoukintei, the independent guest room of the annexe with the exclusive open-air spa

14. The eastern venue, a VIP room in typical Japanese style with a private garden and an open-air spa

Yokikan

Location: 2 – 24, Suehiro-cho, Ito City, Shizuoka, 414-0015, Japan

Spa Name: Ito Onsen

Area: 3,000 m^2

Quantity of Guest Room: 19

Quantity of Spa Bath: 3

Other Facilities: private open-air bath

Located in Suehiro-cho, Ito City, Yokikan had spent the 100th anniversary by July, 2010, since its foundation in Meiji 43 (1910 AD). The one-hundred-year-old hotel takes most pride in its spa facilities (one open-air spa and two indoor spas). It was designed in the elegant environment with beautiful landscapes, occupying the favourable natural terrain of the high hills behind. The mountain trains can take you to the well-known open-air spa and the annexe. The hotel takes pride in its open-air spa with hot springs gushed directly from its properties. Guests may feel like being inside a mountain when entering the central lobby where the waterfall falls vertically among the luxuriant and green trees, creating a dynamic and declicate picture. The two natural hot springs with their own water qualities have different effects. Guests can overlook the Ito Sea and the townscapes of Ito City. It is so quiet and peaceful during nighttime when stars are dotted the whole sky.

Since its foundation, Yokikan has retained its tea house architectural style. There are all together 19 guestrooms built in traditional Japanese style with their own characteristics in three pure Japanese-style buildings on the hillside including the main building, the annexe and Suehirotei. The guests can recuperate themselves in the natural world, being a part of it.

Ito cuisine is always famous for its sea food. Various kinds of cuisine and carefully-made delicacies are cooked with the seasonal local ingredients and seafood selected from the offshore.

2

3

1. The hall – the hotel has retained the tea house architectural style for 100 years since its foundation

2. The vestibule, recuperating in the natural world

3. The dynamic and delicate waterfall falls down in the central lobby

4. The open-air spa commanding a panoramic view of the sea and the whole city

5. The night scene of the spa

6. The vestibule of the pure Japanese-style hotel

4

5

7. The outdoor swimming pool which is only open in summer

8. The after-bath rest area

9. The corridor of "Karei" Bungalou

8

9

10

11

12

10. "Karei" guest room

11. The standard guest room

12. The guest room inside the main building

1

Inatori Ginsuiso

Location: 1624-1, Inatori, Higashiizu-cho, Kamo-gun, Shizuoka Prefecture, 413-0411, Japan

Spa Name: Inatori Onsen

Capacity: 636 persons

Area: 15,370 m^2

Quantity of Guest Room: 117

Quantity of Spa Bath: 4

Other Facilities: outdoor spa with indoor service

Situated in Inatori, Higashiizu-cho, Kamo-gun, Shizuoka-ken, Inatori Ginsui boasts the beautiful scenery of the southland for its ideal location on the east coast of Izu Peninsula close to the Pacific Ocean. Since its foundation in 1957, it has been cherished so much by Japanese people that it has ranked 1st for 16 years in the activity of "Top 100 Japanese Onsens Elected by Experts" host by Japan Travel News Agency. Focusign on the Japanese tradition of hospitality, Inatori Ginsui is a modern Japanese-style hotel welcoming tourists with its own elegance and politeness, showcasing the quintessence of Japanese service.

All guestrooms are oceanfront ones where guests can overlook Izu Shichito Islands and the long beautiful coastline of Izu Peninsula.

There is another outstanding design in Inatori Ginsui – all baths including "Ayame Spa" for men, "Kiou Spa" for women and various open-air bath pools that were designed as "Miyabi kouji", Japanese Ryotei and tea house, and even every rafter were made of Kitayama cedar, which look so luxurious and elegant.

The food served here are the elaortately cooked Iso Ryori (Seafood Feast), coupled with the delicate appearance and considerate service. There are Chinese-speaking waiters and menus in Chinese.

2

3

1. The façade
2. The Japanese Ryotei
3. The night scene of the open-air spa with sea-views
4. The guest room "Zuiun", equipped with high-grade cypress spa
5. The Japanese and Western-style guest room with open-air bath

6. The regular guest room of 11 to 14.5 tatami mats (18 square metres to 24 square metres), with a wide corridor

4

5

Dougashima New Ginsui

Location: 2977 – 1, Nishina, Nishi-Izu-Cho, Kamo-gun, Shizuoka Prefecture, 410-3514, Japan

Spa Name: Inatori Onsen

Area: 49,950 m^2

Quantity of Guest Room: 123

Quantity of Spa Bath: 4

Other Facilities: open-air spa with indoor service

As a sister hotel of Inatori Ginsui, Dougashima new Ginsui is a large-size spa hotel in Dojima, Nishi-Izu-Cho, Kamo-gun, Shizuoka-ken, the famous scenic spot of Nishi-Izu Peninsula. With the basic concept of modern Japansese leisure style, it is a new modern hotel with all-round facilities and top amenities. All guest rooms are ocean fronted, which have a commanding view of the stunning scenery of Dojima and the everchanging coast with ebbs and flows. There are open-air spas, sauna baths and rest areas, where the guest can overlook the greatest scenery of Suruga Bay and Sanshirojima Island. The hot spring swimming pool and other kinds of playgrouns can also be found on the ground floor.

From early October to the first ten days of March next year, guests can admire the stunning scenery of the harmonious amalgamation of the sea and the sky, while enjoying wine drinking (free of charge) on the terrace of Dougashima new ginsui. There are also a large number of tourist attractions and recreational facilities nearby, taking the Dojima Ship as an example, by which the guest can admire the natural picturesque sea cave. Numerous scenic spots and recreational facilities can be seen along the Izu Coastline to Mount Fuji.

The cuisine here is carefully made by the professional Japanese chefs. The menus feature Iso Ryori with abalone or Ise Lobster. There are also Chinese staffs who can offer services in Chinese and moreover, menus in Chinese are available.

1. The façade of the hotel

2. Dojima, also called "Matsushima in Izu" – splendid landscape combining the island on the sea and the coast with cliffs

3. The lighting at the vestibule

4. The exterior scenery

5

5. The façade

3

4

6. The hall

7. The view of the hall from the above

8. The reception hall

7

8

9

10

11

9. The open-air spa
10. The indoor observatory large bath
11. The hall commanding a view of Nishi-Izu

12. The standard Japanese-style guest room with a room area of 14.5 tatami mats and a corridor

13. The Japanese-style guest room

14. The Western-style guest room

13

14

1

Tsubaki

Location: 776 Miyakami, Yugawara-machi, Ashigarashimo-gun, Kanagawa, 259-0314, Japan

Spa Name: Yugawara Onsen

Area: 18,748 m^2

Quantity of Guest Room: 29

Quantity of Spa Bath: 4

Other Facilities: guest room with open-air spa

Nestled in Miyakami,Yugawara-machi, Ashigarashimo-gun, Kanagawa, this striking beauty is found within an hour from the heart of Tokyo by car. The Kabukimon, as well as the cottages of Tsubaki, are built in the Sukiya style, traditional architectural style – characterised by delicate sensibility and ornamented simplicity, in accordance with classic Japanese designing style of Sagano. All buildings are enclosed in Japanese gardens. Covering an area of more than 3000 square metres, the Geihin-kan Pavilion with only five luxurious guestrooms received the best prize of the Kanagawa-Prefecture Architectural Contest in 1985. The main gate, known as Kabukimon, welcomes the guest as a prelude to serene and peaceful visit. The hot spring comes from Yugawara Onsen, which has long been crowned as "Yakushi No Yu". The abundant flow of Tubaki Onsen forms permanent stream all seasons. Lounging in a spacious Grand Hot Spring Spa soothes away daily fatigue and stress. This is the traditional Japanese lifestyle and onsen culture.

Tsubaki is a "Ryotei-Ryokan", a long-history Japanese-style auberge, which features the traditional Japanese Kaiseki cuisine of Kyoto. Guests can enjoy the Kaiseki cuisine made of thin sheets of bean curd, endowed by nature, and then, liying in bed with a soothing heart after enjoying the Japanese food culture.

1. The night view of the façade

2. The façade of the Kyo ryokan consulting the traditional Japanese classic designing style of Sagano

3. The indoor spa bath with permanent flow of hot spring all seasons

4. The VIP room – the Geihin-kan room with Koya Maki open-air spa

5. The VIP room of Geihin-kan

3

4

6. TheJapanese-style guestroom with exclusive spa

7-8. The Geihin-kan room with exclusive open-air spa bath

7
8

9

10

11

9. Zen Style SPA ichirin in which you can enjoy the utmost comfort

10. The salon bar "Shu-chu-ka" surrounded by gardens

11. The exclusive spa bath in the Japanese and Western-style guestroom

12. The guest room in Japanese and Western style with exclusive open-air spa

13. The guest room of Geihin-kan

14. The Japanese and Western-style guest room

13

14

Sansuirou

Location: 673, Miyakami, Yugawara, Asigarasimogun, Kanagawa Prefecture, 259-0314, Japan

Spa Name: Yugawara Onsen

Area: 3,622 m²

Quantity of Guest Room: 57

Quantity of Spa Bath: 4

Other Facilities: guest room with open-air spa

Located in Yugawara, Asigarasimogun, Kanagawa Prefecture, Sansuirou and Tubaki are two hotels of the same company yet with their own characteristics. Sansuirou has been crowned as Mini Kyoto of Sagami since its foundation in Shouwa 8 (1933) and was chosen as one of the "250 Most Popular Onsen Ryokans with 5-star Accomation Facilities" in 2010. All of the four complexes "Jurakudai", "Jyobandai", the annexe "Genji" and "Momayamadai" of Sansuirou have a broad view for its high-level terrain (there are even open-air spa pool on the seventh floor), commanding a panoramic view of the green water of Fujiki River, while the starry sky is more remarkable as the stars are so close that is even reachable with hands,

Upon entering from the vestibule, then the reception desk and the corridor, guests are blessed with a surene and peaceful mind within the spacious room with gentle light. Each and every guest room is designed with their own view of landscapes such as varied and graceful trees and jungles, the beautiful scenery of Somma and the clear stream of Fujiki River. The hot spring here all come from Yugawara Onsen. There are not only indoor open-air spas but also the observatory large communal spa named "Ozora", making guests fully intoxicated in the amorous feelings endowed by nature. Moreover, wormwood fumigation service is also available here. Guests can enjoy traditional Kaiseki cuisine in guest rooms of pure Japanese style.

1. The façade of the hotel

2. The exclusive open-air spa of the luxury guest room "Momoyamadai"

3. The vestibule – the entrance

4. The corridor

5. The hall of the hotel in the style of Kyoto Ryotei Ryokan

3

4

6

7

8

6. The observatory open-air spa "Ozora", with a commanding view of the natural scene of Okuyugawara

7. The exclusive open-air spa of the luxury guest room "Momoyamadai"

8. The indoor large bath in which you can admire the beautiful Japanese garden

9

10

11

9. The beauty salon "Madoromi SPA SUI"

10. The exclusive terrace of the guest room "Jyobandai"

11. The Japanese-style guest room "Jyobandai"

12

13

14

12. The dressing room of luxury guest room "Momoyamadai"

13. The luxury guest room "Momoyamadai", Japanese style with an area of 16 tatami mats (26 square metres)

14. The guest room named "Momoyamadai" with 16 tatami mats, Western-style bed room, a dressing room, an indoor bath pool and an open-air spa

Seiransou

Location: 679, Miyakami, Yugawara, Asigarasimogun, Kanagawa Prefecture, 259-0314, Japan

Spa Name: Yugawara Onsen

Quantity of Guest Room: 48

Quantity of Spa Bath: 5

Other Facilities: guest room with open-air spa, rentable spa

Located in Yugawara, Asigarasimogun, which is only 90 minutes' walk from Tokyo, Seiransou is an historic and famous onsen hotel with a history of more than 80 years. With graceful natural scenery, Oku-Yugawara is a county park in Kanagawa Prefecture, which has a long history since its foundation in Shouwa Age, while many historical sites of that time can still be found now. The vermeil wooden bridge stretching across the opposite Hakuryu Waterfall, which falls from 38 metres above. Seiransou is characterised by a vivid picture of wild phenomena such as the wriggling Hakuryu Waterfall next to the guestrooms, the open-air spa surrounded by wonderful mountains and stones in odd shapes. Guests can sooth their hearts as a part of the green mountains and the blue water while listening to the artistic rippling song of the running water. It was the blue sky and the green mountains that gave birth to the name of the hotel.

The two hot springs here all comes from its own property. The water temperature is kept at 70 degree to 80 degree with a gushing volume of 100 litres per minute. The indoor spas also use the circulating hot spring. The water in the spa has chloride and vitoriol elements, which boasts the quality of alkalescence and hypotonicity. Transparent and free from extraneous odour, the hot water makes guests feel comfortable with its constant temperature, producing a significant effect in curing neuralgia, osphyalgia and gynaecopathia.

1. The open-air spa commanding a view of the waterfall
2. The façade of the garden of the annexe
3. The paradise-like open-air spa

4. The vermeil bridge to the open-air spa

5

6

5. The open-air spa for women
6. The indoor spa for men
7. The paradise-like open-air spa

8. The outdoor bathing place in the annexe (available 24 hours)

9. Women's spa (available 24 hours)

10. The banquet hall

11. A special guest room in the annexe

12. Japanese-style guest room in the annexe (16 square metres) with its own bathroom

13. Japanese-style guest room in the main building (16 square metres) with its own bathroom

12

13

1

Onyadomegumi

Location: 361 Miyakami, Yugawara-machi, Ashigarashimo-gun, Kanagawa Prefecture, 259-0314, Japan

Spa Name: Yugawara Onsen

Area: 2,848 m^2

Quantity of Guest Room: 37

Quantity of Spa Bath: 4

Other Facilities: private open-air spa, 2 rentable spa, foot spa

Enjoying the ideal location of the central area of Yugawara Onsen in Yugawara-machi, Ashigarashimo-gun, Kanagawa Prefecture and the convenient transportation, Onyadomegumi is a famous spa and health resort in Japan. To realise the concept of "Megumi" (affluence and happiness), it is a typical modern architecture combining the ancient and modern designing techniques. Besides its indurative shatter-proof structure, the main building "Seseragi-Kan" founded in 1995 and the annexe "Tsuki no takumi" also incorporates the merits of buildings in Edo era. A foot spa is designed in the atrium for guests to have a warm and comfortable foot spa. The women's open-air spa "Ebisu-No-Yu" is made of granite, whose tone and thickness demonstrate fully the artistic effect of the natural stone. The men's open-air spa "Bishamon-No-Yu", which was decorated by Libanotis buchtormensis made of granite and the bamboo curtain, looks extraordinarily simple and antique. Facing the garden and the mountains, the private chartered bath "Ginga" creates a feeling of openness, while evokes mysterious dream with its grand vision at night when plants and flowers in the garden are illuminated by lights.

Taking guests' diversified requirements into account, all the facilities here are barrier free design, which guarantee a comfort and cosy living environment for guests.

1. The foot spa designed uniquely in the atrium, feet relax in the gentle hot spring while admiring the flowers and plants in the midnight light, the wonderful garden scenery

2. The façade of the tile-roofed building, designed with the prototype of shops in Edo period

3. Men's open-air spa "Bishamon-No-Yu", made of andesite

4. Women's open-air spa "Ebisu-No-Yu", made of andesite, whose tone and thickness demonstrate fully the artistic effect of natural stone

5. The spacious hall with historic taste

3

4

6. Men's indoor spa "Bishamon-No-Yu" with high-grade cypress as the decorative material for fringe

7. Women's indoor spa "Ebisu-No-Yu" is made of andesite

8. The exclusive open-air spa in the Japanese-style guest room

7

8

9

10

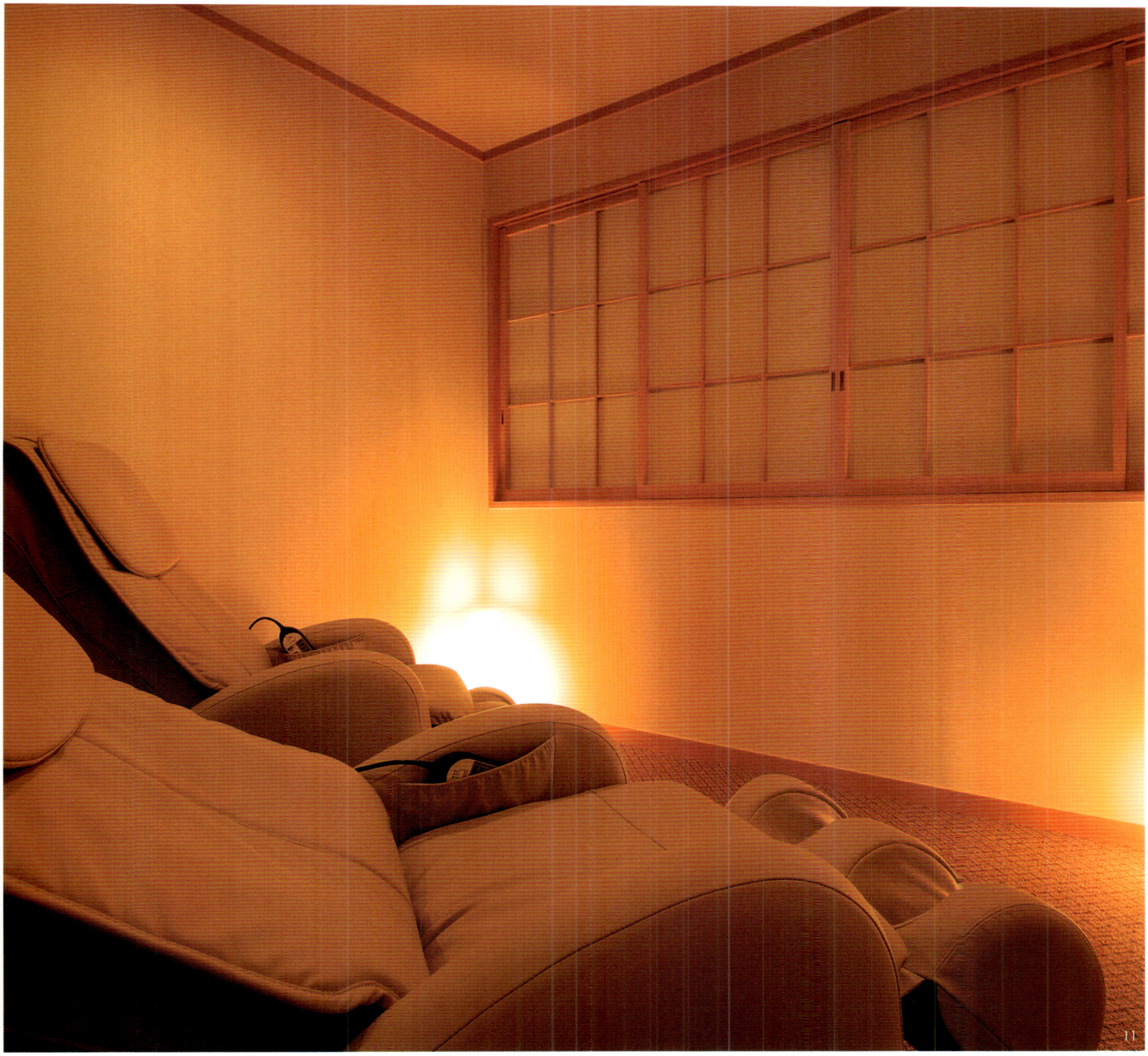

9. The chartered spa bath "Ginga" facing the garden and the mountain with a sense of openness

10. The panorama of the Japanese and Western-style guest room with exclusive open-air spa on the outdoor terrace, covering a total area of 87 square metres

11. The rest area equipped with two massage armchairs

12. The Japanese-style guest room with exclusive open-air spa, made of tuff

13. The dinning room in the Japanese-style guest room with exclusive open-air spa

14. The Japanese and Western-style guest room with exclusive open-air spa on the outdoor terrace, covering a total area of 67 square metres

13

14

Mikawaya Ryokan

Location: 503 Kowakidani, Hakone-machi, Ashigarashimo-gun, Kanagawa, 250-0406, Japan

Spa Name: Kowakidani Onsen

Area: 66,000 m^2

Quantity of Guest Room: 35

Quantity of Spa Bath: 6

Other Facilities: guest room with indoor open-air spa, rentable spa

Seated in Kowakidani Mountain, Hakone-machi, Ashigarashimo-gun, Kanagawa, approximately 600 metres above sea level, Mikawaya Ryokan is an old brand with a building history of more than 10 decades since its foundation in Meiji 16 (1883 AD). It is not only an elegant and graceful hotel, the central meaning of its theme "Fuga", but also a resort full of rich historical stories. The great pioneer of the democratic revolution of China, Sun Yat-sen has enjoyed his stay here in the guest room named "Shochiku", where the writing of Mr. Sun's "High Mountains and Floating Water" is still carefully kept here. It is also favoured by many Japanese poets and writers, among whom the famous Japanese drawer Yumeji Takehisa left his great work "Tanabata" (The Star Festival), which is hung at the vestibule, after enjoying his stay here. Moreover, it is the refuge of numerous superstars, filmstars and writers. The lounge in the style of Taisho period can still be seen in the hotel.

The guest rooms with open-air spa named "Kasumi" and "Tsutsuji" put together all graceful elements of the traditional Japanese ryokan. The large bath "Meji", with a long history and culture, inherits the romantic charm of Meji period. Guests can enjoy the bathing while admiring the grand scenery of the ever-changing natural landscape in different seasons: sakura and cuckoo in spring, lilium brownii in summer, red maple leaves in autumn and the snow-covered landscape in winter – the Eastern way of life that men and the nature live in harmony is incisively and vividly demonstrated here. The simple alkaline hot spring has a significant curative effect in skincare with little mineral substance and less durability.

1. The outdoor view which can be overlooked from the guest room (in April), the broad garden in the simple and elegant colour of cherry blossom

2. The garden in summer – as the affiliated garden, Houraien boasts the enchanting scenery changing with seasons.

3. The façade of the Japanese-style hotel with a history of 10 decades

4

4. The façade

5

5. The vestibule permeated with a sense of history

6. The corridor inside

7. The independent guest room "Hanare", the guest room "TSUTSUJI" with open-air spa on the terrace and a private garden with blooming sakura (the first and middle ten days of April)

8. The large bath "Meiji"

9

10

9. The large bath "Meiji"

10. Men's open-air spa

11. The stairs to the guestroom "Sho chiku"

12

13

14

12. The guest room "Sho chiku", where you can overlook the outdoor garden on the terrace

13. The guest room "Sho chiku", where the great Chinese leader Sun Yat-sen had stayed

14. The guest room with open-air spa named "Kasumi"

1

Hakone Hotel Kowakien

Location: 1297 Ninotaira Hakone-machi, Ashigarashimo-gun, Kanagawa-ken, 250-0407, Japna

Spa Name: Kowakidani Onsen

Area: 16,000 m^2

Quantity of Guest Room: 220

Quantity of Spa Bath: 4

Located in Ninotaira Hakone-machi, Ashigarashimo-gun, Kanagawa-ken, the most popular tourist attraction in Japan, Hakone Hotel Kowakien enjoys a long history and moreover wins the great affection from people at home and abroad in that its hot spring (spring water is rich in beneficial mineral substances), as gentle as astringent, has the special efficacy to skincare. Covering an area of 16,000 square metres, it is a recreation centre focusing on the theme of onsen. There are various kinds of baths within the five onsen areas with their own themes such as the wine onsen, the coffee onsen, the most outstanding one – the miraculous Dead Sea Onsen and the traditional Japanese onsen "Mori no Yu", which combines the magnificence of Hakone and the glamour of nature together. Surrounded by beautiful natural scenery, "Mori No Yu" is the largest open-air spa in Hakone, whose marvelous space design affords guests a panoramic view of the vasty garden and the splendid scenery of Hakone Somma.

Appetising dishes from across the world are served in the five dinning rooms of the hotel, such as Japanese Kaiseki Cuisine, the superior Mediterranean Cuisine, Teppangaki and the like.

1. The night scene of the façade

2. The open-air spa "Mori no Yu", the largest hot spring bath in Hakone

3. The open-air wine spa

4. The standard twin room – there are so many accommodation choices here with considerate services from the standard double-bed room to the elegant royal suites

5. The terrace of the guest room, which commands a panoramic view of the broad garden and the splendid landscape of Hakone Somma

3

4

Hotel ChooBoo Sansou

Location: 698-25 Miyashita, Yugawara, Asigarasimogun, Kanagawa Prefecture, 259-0304, Japan

Spa Name: Yugawara Onsen

Area: 9,000 m²

Quantity of Guest Room: 6

Quantity of Spa Bath: 3

Other Facilities: rentable spa

Built on the hathpace near Yugawara Station, Hotel ChooBoo enjoys the ideal location in Yugawara Onsen Town in Yugawara, Asigarasimogun, Kanagawa Prefecture. Taking full advantage of the ideal geographical position with a long history and particularly favourable natural condition, it creates a surreal world for guests, being a part of nature. Just as the meaning implied by the hotel name, the designer aimed to build a hotel on the hathpace, which has a commanding view of infinite scenes. Guests can enjoy the cosy and comfortable onsens here while more importantly, overlook the sky, blue sea, the lush forest on mountains far away, the pretty neighbourhood and the winding Hydra-like Shinkansen, feeling like being integrated in the sky. The typical Western and Japanese-style buildings against the background of all these wonderful scenes make guests feel better than the lively supernatural beings.

The natural alkaline hot spring has the bubble massage function. There are various kinds of cuisine served here, the Western style and the Japanese style, which can be chosen by personal habit.

1. The façade
2. The open-air spa
3. The surrounding scenic spots
4. The large spa pool with the function of bubble massage

5 The surrounding scenic spots

3

4

6. The large spa with the function of bubble massage

7. The guest room in unique style

8. The double-bed room in Western style, with a panoramic view of the seascape

7

8

Yugawara Mizunokaori

Location: 614 Miyakami, Yugawara-machi, Ashigarashimo-gun, Kanagawa Prefecture, 259-0314, Japan

Spa Name: Yugawara Onsen

Area: 1,421 m^2

Quantity of Guest Room: 25

Quantity of Spa Bath: 4

Other Facilities: private open-air spa

Nestled in Miyakami, Yugawara-machi, Ashigarashimo-gun, Kanagawa Prefecture, it was built along the river with rippling water and rolling stream. The hot spring, coming from its own properties, can make skin soft, moist and smooth, and the gentle water quality without any irritating substances is suitable for children. Guests can soothe their hearts in the bright and spacious large spa in their favourite bathrobes. However, the open-air spa endow guests with more interests and pleasure. From the early morning to the midnight, guests can feel the same natural beauty and amorous feelings but different joyness brought by the changing time. The standard guest room with an area of 17 square metres has a commanding view beautiful scenes of Yugawara – the picturesque overlapping mountains and green trees, tranquil and peaceful.

It is only takes10 minutes to walk from the hotel to Manyo Park, where guests enjoying foot spa while admiring diversified sceneries in four seasons such as the fireflies all over the garden in summer and the fiery-red maple leaves in autumn.

The Japanese Kaiseki Cuisine, made of fresh seasonal ingredients, has won good reputation among guests. There is also delicate coffee for guests. All the thoughtful service leaves guests unforgettable memories.

1. The façade of the hotel with a creek trickling sluggishly nearby

2. Gentlemen's observatory open-air spa where you can overlook the stunning scenery of Yugawara while enjoying birds' tweedle

3. Ladies' observatory open-air spa within the environment of rolling and overlapping mountains with lush trees

4. The restaurant. Guest can choose to dine in the restaurant or in the guest room

5. The indoor spa, the rock bathroom

3

4

6

6. The standard Japanese-style guest room with an area of 17 square metres, where you can enjoy the natural beauty and tranquility of Yugawara

7. The barrier free guest room designed for the elder and disabled

1

Hotel Shiroyama

Location: 207 Shirohori, Yugawara-machi, Ashigarashimo-gun, Kanagawa Prefecture, 259-0314, Japan

Spa Name: Yugawara Onsen

Area: 1,152.42 m^2

Quantity of Guest Room: 20

Quantity of Spa Bath: 4

Other Facilities: guest room with open-air spa, rentable spa

It is only two minutes' walk from Yugawara Tram Stop to Hotel Shiroyama, located in Shirohori, Yugawara-machi, Ashigarashimo-gun, Kanagawa Prefecture. Hotel Shiroyama and Yugawara Mizunokaori are two chain hotels with different names and characteristics. Yugawara Onsen can be divided into two types according to the different qualities: the meek and smooth natural hot spring and the hot spring with rich minerals. To meet guests' requirements of multiaspects, some guest rooms underwent redecoration in July, 2007 when the Japanese-style guest rooms with open-air spa, Japanese and Western-style guest rooms, double-bed rooms were added. There are also large Japanese-style rooms which can accommodate eight persons, guest rooms with open-air spa named "Aoi" and "Koutou" and the Western-style guest rooms named "Shinonome".

The restaurant features seasonal "Hana Kaiseki Zen", cooked with the fresh marine fish from the nearby sea and local vegetables and fruits. Moreover, guests can choose their own favoured menus such as the roast meat cuisine and the Kaiseki Ryori with abalone and Ise lobster. The family guests or travelling couples can enjoy their dinner with leisure in their rooms.

1. The rentable open-air spa

2. The open-air spa of the guest room "Koutou"

3-4. The spacious Japanese-style guest room which can accommodate eight persons

5. The guest room "Aoi" with open-air spa

6. The guest room "Koutou" with open-air spa

7. The western-style guest room named "Shinonome"

6
7

1

Prince Hotel Manza

Location: Manza Onsen, Tsumagoi-mura, Agatsumagun, Gunma Prefecture, 377-1595, Japan

Spa Name: Manza Onsen

Area: 34,957 m^2

Quantity of Guest Room: 232

Quantity of Spa Bath: open-air spa 6, indoor spa 4

Prince Hotel Manza is located in Tsumagoi-mura Resorts, Agatsumagun, Gunma Prefecture. Manza Onsen has been crowned as "Onsen Beyond the Clouds" and "Onsen Closest to the Starry Sky", as it is the highest onsen that can be reached by trolley bus, located on Mt. Shirane, 1,800 metres above sea level. Manza Onsen is one of the best onsens in Japan for its ideal location in the environment the same like the three terrains with the longest longevity in the world. It is also worldwide-known for its abundant hot spring volume. The 27 kinds of minerals and trace elements contained in the milky white water have many effects, which have been described as the catholicon that can cure all diseases and has been favoured by women for its efficacy in skincare. Available 24 hours, there are women's exclusive spas, men's exclusive spas and the mixed ones. In the spacious onsen named "Komasaku" with the thorough openness, guests can experience various feelings in different seasons such as the green and fresh spring, the cool summer with gentle breeze, the affluent autumn with red maple leaves and the silver white winter. Guests may also soothe their bodies and mind by enjoying the two kinds of natural spas in "Ishiniwa Open-air Spa" – the white turbid hot spring spa and the yellow turbid hot spring spa, on the highland in the starry sky.

2

3

1. The façade of the hotel in autumn

2. The autumn scenery of the open-air spa "Komasaku" of Prince Hotel Manza

3. The open-air spa "Komakusa" of Prince Hotel Manza

4. The summer scenery of "Ishiniwa Open-air Spa" of Prince Hotel Manza

5. The open-air spa "Komakusa" of Prince Hotel Manza – the top Takayama hot spring locates 1,800 metres high above sea level, which is called "Onsen Beyond the Clouds"

6. The winter scenery of the open-air spa "Komasaku"

標高一、八〇〇M雲上の露天風呂

7

7. The night scene of "Ishiniwa Open-air Spa" of Prince Hotel Manza

8. The beauty salon, SPA

9. The Western-style guest room

8

9

Index

Kanagawa Prefecture

Hakone Onsen

1. Mikawaya Ryokan
   503 Kowakidani, Hakone-machi, Ashigarashimo-gun, Kanagawa Prefecture, 250-0406, Japan
   http://www.hakone-mikawaya.com/

2. Gora Tensui
   1320-276 Gora, Hakone, Asigarasimo-gun, Kanagawa Prefecture, Japan
   http://www.gora-tensui.com/

3. Hotel Kajikaso
   688 Yumoto, Hakone-machi, Ashigarashimo-gun, Kanagawa Prefecture, Japan
   http://www.kajikaso.co.jp/

4. Yushintei
   193 Yumoto, Ashigarashimo-gun, Kanagawa Prefecture, Japan
   http://www.yushintei.co.jp/

5. Hakone Hougetu
   90-42 Hakone, Hakone, Asigarasimo-gun, Kanagawa Prefecture, 250-0522, Japan
   http://hakone-hougetu.com/

6. The Prince Hakone
   144 Motonhakone, Hakone-machi, Ashigara-shimo-gun, Kanagawa Prefecture, 250-0592, Japan
   http://www.princehotels.co.jp/the_prince_hakone

7. Hakone Hotel Kowakien
   1297 Ninotaira Hakone-machi, Ashigarashimo-gun, Kanagawa Prefecture, 250-0407, Japan
   http://www.hakoneho-kowakien.com/

Yugawara Onsen

8. Tubaki
   776 Miyakami, Yugawara-machi, Ashigarashimo-gun, Kanagawa Prefecture, 259-0314, Japan
   http://www.tubaki.net/

9. Sansuirou
   673, Miyakami, Yugawara, Asigarasimo-gun, Kanagawa Prefecture, 259-0314, Japan
   http://www.sansuirou.cc.jp/

10. Hotel ChooBoo
    698-25 Miyashita, Yugawara, Asigarasimo-gun, Kanagawa Prefecture, 259-0304, Japan
    http://www.chooboo.co.jp/

11. Onyadomegumi
    361 Miyakami, Yugawara-machi, Ashigarashimo-gun, Kanagawa Prefecture, 259-0314, Japan
    http://www.onyadomegumi.co.jp/

12. Ootaki Hotel
    750-1 Miyakami, Yugawara-machi, Ashigarashimo-gun, Kanagawa Prefecture, 259-0314, Japan
    http://www.ootaki-hotel.com/

13. Yugawara Mizunokaori
    614 Miyakami, Yugawara-machi, Ashigarashimo-gun, Kanagawa Prefecture, 259-0314, Japan
    http://www.mizunokaori.com/

14. Hotel Shiroyama
    207 Shirohori, Yugawara-machi, Ashigarashimo-gun, Kanagawa Prefecture, 259-0314, Japan
    http://www.hotel-shiroyama.com/

15. Seiransou
    679, Miyakami, Yugawara, Asigarasimogun, Kanagawa Prefecture, 259-0314, Japan
    http://www.seiransou.co.jp/

Shizuoka Prefecture

Atami Onsen

16. Horai
    750-6 Mount Ito, Atami, Shizuoka Prefecture, 413-0002, Japan
    http://www.izusan-horai.com

17. Otsuki Hotel Wafuukan
    3-19 Higashikaigancho, Atami, Shizuoka Prefecture,413-0012, Japan
    http://www.wafuukan.com/

18. Hotel MICURAS
    3-19, Higashikaigancho, Atami, Shizuoka Prefecture, 413-0012, Japan
    http://www.micuras.jp/ http://www.orix.co.jp/grp/content/070119_MicurasJ.pdf

19. Atami Sakuraya Ryokan
    9-11 Higashikaigancho, Atami-shi, Shizuoka Prefecture, 413-0012, Japan
    http://www.atami-sakuraya.com/

20. Sun Hatoya
    572-12, Yukawa, Ito City, Shizuoka Prefecture, 414-0002, Japan
    http://www.sunhatoya.co.jp/home/index.html

21. Hotel Hatoya
    1391 Oka, Ito City, Shizuoka Prefecture 414-0055, Japan
    http://www.hatoyahotel.com/home/

22. Laforet Club Hotel Yitou
    2-3-1 Shishido, Ito City, Shizuoka Prefecture, 414-0004, Japan
    http://www.laforet.co.jp/lfhotels/ito/

23. Yokikan
    2-24, Suehiro-cho, Ito City, Shizuoka Prefecture, 414-0015, Japan
    http://www.yokikan.co.jp

24. IDUMISOU
    2-21 Okahiro-cho, Ito City, Shizuoka Prefecture, 414-0016, Japan
    http://www.idumisou.co.jp

25. ANGINE
    5-12 Nagisa-cho, Ito City, Shizuoka Prefecture, 414-0023, Japan
    http://www.angine.jp

26. Zagyosoh
    1741, Yawatano, Ito City, Shizuoka Prefecture, Japan
    http://www.zagyosoh.com/index.html

27. HANAFUBUKI Ryokan
    1041 Yawata, Ito City, Shizuoka Prefecture,413-0232, Japan
    http://www.hanafubuki.co.jp/kantai/index.htm

28. Southern Cross Resort Hotel
    1006 Yoshida, Ito City, Shizuoka Prefecture, 414-0051, Japan
    http://www.southerncross.co.jp/

29. Seizanyamato
    203 Oka, Ito-City Shizouka Prefecture, 414-0055, Japan
    http://www.seizanyamato.jp/

Shuizenji Onsen

30. Sora Togetsusou Kinryu
    3455 Shuizenji, Izu City, Shizuoka Prefecture, 410-2416, Japan
    http://www.kinryu.net/

31. Yagyu-no-Sho
    1116-6, Shuzenji, Izu City, Shizuoka Prefecture, 410-2416, Japan
    http://www.yagyu-no-sho.com/

32. ASABA Ryokan
    3450-1, Shuzenji, Ito-shi, Shizuoka Prefecture,Japan
    http://goriben.com/ryokan_desc.php?code=Asaba&pft=Shizuok\

33. Inatori Ginsui
    1624-1, Inatori, Higashiizu-cho, Kamo-gun, Shizuoka Prefecture, 413-0411, Japan
    http://www.inatori-ginsuiso.jp/

34. Dougashima New Ginsui
    2977-1, Nishina, Nishi-Izu-Cho, Kamo-gun, Shizuoka Prefecture, 410-3514, Japan
    http://www.dougashima-newginsui.jp/

Toi Onsen

35. Mizuniwa no Hatago Sumiyoshikan
    1149-1, Kona, Izunokuni -city, Shizuoka Prefecture, 410-2201, Japan
    http://www.sumiyosikan.com/

36. Nishiizu Toi Onsen Hotel Miyabi
    241 Nishiizu Toi, Izu, Shizuoka Prefecture, 410-3301, Japan
    http://www.toi-miyabi.com/

37. Toi Hotel Sankaitei
    324 Toi, Ito-city, Shizuoka Prefecture, 410-3302, Japan
    http://www.toi-sankaitei.com/

Amagi Yujima Onsen

38. Ochiairou Murakami
    1887-1 Yujima, Izu, Shizuoka Prefecture, 410-3206, Japan
    http://www.ochiairou.com/

39. Amagisou
    359 Nashimoto, Kawazu-cho, Kamo-gun, Shizuoka Prefecture, Japan
    http://www.amagisou.jp/

Kanznjicho Onsen

40. Hotel Hananoi
    399-1 Kanznjicho, West District, Hamamatsu, Shizuoka Prefecture, 431-1209, Japan
    http://www.hananoi.com/

Shimoda Onsen

41. Shimoda Yamatokan
    2048 Kisami, Shimoda, Shizuka Prefecture, 415-0028, Japan
    http:// www.shimoda-yamatokan.co.jp/

42. Hotel Izukyu
    2732-7 Shirahama, Shimoda, Shizuoka Prefecture, 415-8512, Japan
    http://www.hotel-izukyu.co.jp/index.html

Yamanashi Prefecture

Isawa Onsen

43. Isawa View Hotel
    Nakajima 1607, Isawa-cho, Fuefuki City, Yamanashi Prefecture, 406-0024, Japan
    http://www.i-view.jp/

44. Hotel Hana-isawa
    Matsumoto 1409 Isawa-cho, Fuefuki City, Yamanashi Prefecture, 406-0021, Japan
    http://www.i-view.jp/
    http://www.hana-isawa.com/language/ch_h/

45. Kasugai View Hotel
    Shizume 178, Kasugai-cho, Fuefuki-City, Yamanashi Prefecture, 406-0021, Japan
    http://www.k-view.jp/language/ch_k/index.html

Chiba Prefecture

Kamogawakan Onsen

46. Ryokan Kamogawakan
    1179 Nishi-cho, Kamogawa City, Chiba Prefecture, Japan
    http://www.japan-ryokan.net/kamogawakan/zh-CN/index.html

Hoshino Onsen

47. Hoshinoya Karuizawa
    Hoshino, Karuizawa-machi, Nagano Prefecture, 339-0194, Japan
    http://www.hoshinoya.com/

Asama Onsen

48. Kishoan
    1-31-1, Matsumoto City, Nagano Prefecture, 390-0303, Japan
    http://www.kishoan.net

49. Laforet Club Hotel Naka-Karuizawa
    4339 Nagakura, Karuizawa-machi, Kitasaku-gun, Nagano Prefecture, 325-0301, Japan
    http://www.laforet.co.jp/lfhotels/krz/index.html

Tochigi Prefecture

New Nasu Onsen

50. Hotel Laforet Nasu
    206-959, Yumoto, Nasu-machi, Nasu-gun, Tochigi Prefecture,325-0301, Japan
    http://www.laforet.co.jp/lfhotels/nas/index.html

Gunma Prefecture

Manza Onsen

51. Prince Hotel Manza
    Manza Onsen, Tsumagoi-mura, Agatsumagun, Gunma Prefecture, 377-1595, Japan
    http://www.princehotels.co.jp/manza/

This edition published in September 2011

Design Media Publishing Limited
20/F Manulife Tower
169 Electric Rd, North Point
Hong Kong
Tel: 00852-28672587
Fax: 00852-25050411
E-mail: Kevinchoy@designmediahk.com
www.designmediahk.com

Editing: Jinling Qu
English Translation: Weinan Dai
Proofreading: Qian Yin
Design/Layout: Coraline Cao

ISBN 978-988-15071-6-7

Printed in China